ONE IN A SERIES FROM THE PUBLISHERS OF *PRE-K TODAY*

LEARNING THROUGH PLAY
COOKING

A Practical Guide for Teaching Young Children

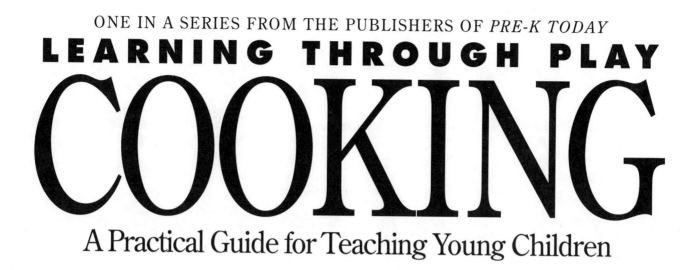

Written by Lisa Feeney

Foreword by Bonnie Blagojević

Contributing Writers:

Ellen Booth Church

Merle Karnes, Ed.D.

Kathie Spitzley

Constance Ward

Illustrated by Nicole Rubel

Early Childhood Division Vice President and Publisher

Helen Benham

Art Director

Toby Fox

Production Editor

Katie Lyons

Editor

Jane Schall

Associate Editor

Ilene S. Rosen

Activity Plans written by

Ellen Booth Church,

Lisa Feeney, and Constance Ward

Copyright © 1992 by Scholastic Inc.

Published by:
Scholastic Inc.
Early Childhood Division
730 Broadway
New York, NY 10003

ISBN # 0-590-49246-2
Library of Congress Catalog Number

W9-AEG-219

CONTENTS

LEARNING AND GROWING WITH COOKING

ACTIVITY PLANS
FOR TWOS, THREES, FOURS, AND FIVES

Cover Photo: James Levin

- 4 -

THIS BOOK IS DEDICATED TO
ROSE CIFFOLILLO,
WHO TAUGHT ME THAT COOKING
AND LOVE ARE SYNONYMOUS.

— Lisa Feeney

FOREWORD
A Conversation with Bonnie Blagojević

Bonnie, could you explain how creativity fits into a group experience like cooking?

I started cooking with young children 10 years ago, when I began working in day-care programs. But recently I've come to realize that just as there are product-versus-process experiences in art, cooking projects that allow children to make choices and express themselves individually are more fun and exciting than ones in which everything turns out the same.

Just as in your program, "We Knead Mondays"?

Yes. That all began about two years ago, on a Monday, when one of my three-year-olds walked in, put his hands on his hips and declared, "I am angry." That same morning, one of the five-year-olds was arguing with her friend while other children who normally played together happily were irritable and edgy. Both Cindy, the woman who works with me, and I, felt battle weary — as if we were just keeping the peace instead of enjoying the children.

Upon reflection, we realized that Monday mornings tended to be unsettling. And as I thought about it, it made sense. Children (and adults!) have to shift gears after the weekend as they move back into a setting that involves the wants and needs of many individuals, not just their own. Plus, children ranging in age from two to five years have varying abilities to express how they feel. I couldn't change the circumstances, but there had to be a way to help children re-enter their day-care world comfortably. I knew that their emotions and energy needed outlets; that they needed to feel accepted and comfortable in their group again.

I hit on the idea of making bread — and it worked. Early Monday morning, I would mix up yeasted bread dough. As children arrived, we'd invite them to come help. Where does the creativity fit in? Each child could make his or her own small loaf, using individual kneading techniques that would range from vicious pummeling to a pound-and-snooze approach. The smells and textures of the dough got imaginative juices flowing, resulting in a variety of designs and shapes.

And you've expanded?

Yes. The more we explored bread making, the more exciting discoveries we made. For instance, baking bread can suit particular moods. Children might come in with the end-of-the-winter blahs. That can happen in Maine, when April arrives and we continue to wait for that glimmer of sunshine and warmth. So on one of those days when spring just seemed too far away, I decided we'd make pink bread using beets. There's one child I have who comes late and doesn't usually choose baking, but that day I think everyone was involved, working with the dough for about 45 minutes. Another time, two brothers decided they were going to shape all the breads they made into slugs — a whole family of slugs.

Because children are able to express themselves through cooking and come up with their own creations, they feel empowered and want to participate. You see, cooking is a process, a creative outlet for the individual child. At the same time, working side by side builds feelings of warmth, security, and camaraderie. Children get that important sense of belonging and contributing to the group. In the end, there we all are, having snack together at my big dining room table, filled with a sense of pride and satisfaction at the tasty creations we prepared in the company of friends.

There are so many skills involved in cooking experiences.

Yes, but besides curriculum-area skills, one of the things we try to foster through cooking is making choices. For instance, I might take a healthy food like a kiwi and say, "What are we going to do with this?" "What could we make?" Or take carrot wheels and celery and let children design their own snacks. We call everything they make creations because they make the choices.

And when children make choices ...

They feel good. They have power over the process and over the product. If they use their imaginations to make slug bread, they've decided what to do with that bread. They're controlled so much, because they're small — what they need are chances to feel powerful.

Children are so incredibly inventive. So if you get bored with snack, set out some ingredients — cottage cheese, fruits, maybe crackers — and let children choose. Ask them to suggest healthy foods. Provide them, and let children decide how to combine them. They come up with ideas we would never even think about. Opportunities to make choices lead to practicing thinking skills.

There's a sense of adventure in cooking: It's fun, and it's a wonderful source for childhood memories.

Bonnie Blagojević has a master's degree in elementary education; operates Morningtown Childcare, a mixed-age family day-care home in Orono, Maine; and is a free-lance writer.

COOKING IS A GREAT EXPERIENCE

If you could design the ideal preschool activity, what would it be? An activity that inherently motivates and challenges children? One that offers real opportunities for social, emotional, intellectual, and physical development? One that invites children to experience math, science, social studies, and language learning? An activity that calls on their creativity and all of their senses? One that's fun for everyone? This might seem to be an impossibly tall order to fill. But many early childhood professionals agree that cooking with young children answers all of these needs, and even more. When carefully planned and thoughtfully presented, cooking is a wonderfully rewarding preschool experience.

COOKING IS HIGHLY MOTIVATING

Simply by its nature, cooking calls out to children to participate and follow through. Young children are familiar with food and most have had pleasurable experiences with it at home. They have few fears or trepidations about getting involved with, investigating, and manipulating ingredients and equipment. And most young children get excited about the chance to perform real tasks — not pretending to do, but actually doing. Cooking is also an activity adults can get excited about, and their enthusiasm is surely conveyed to the children around them.

COOKING PROVIDES OPPORTUNITIES TO GROW

Children grow socially as they share and cooperate, working together toward a common (edible) goal. They may become aware of others' needs as they wait their turn and share foods with other children. They experience individual differences in preference and taste.

Emotionally, children have the opportunity to experience a range of positive feelings when they cook. Slicing apples for fruit salad may help children feel competent as they attempt and then master a new skill. Children develop a sense of autonomy as they work independently, and self-confidence as they make choices to create a product uniquely their own. Feelings of pride and accomplishment flow as children complete their tasks, then share their creations with others.

Physically, cooking offers preschool-aged children opportunities to develop large- and small-muscle control as they roll, pinch, knead, pat, spread, cut, stir, shake, pour, and scrub.

Cognitively, growth occurs when children use all of their senses. They touch, taste, smell, see, and even hear while they experience the properties and changes involved in various ingredients and procedures. When children cook their own food, they are truly active learners making sense of their world.

COOKING CROSSES CURRICULUM BOUNDARIES

As you know, children learn best from real experiences. Cooking is just that — an experience that integrates all areas of learning.

■ Cooking is math when children cut foods into parts, measure, weigh, count, sort, use timers, and estimate ingredients; use one-to-one correspondence to mete out foods and utensils; recognize shapes and sizes of foods; and use charts and graphs to keep track of favorites, varieties, and even timing.

■ Cooking is science when children question, experiment, investigate, observe, predict, and draw conclusions; grow plants to use in cooking; observe the heating and cooling of foods; and combine individual ingredients to make a new whole.

■ Cooking is social studies when children work cooperatively, share, solve problems, and experience similarities and differences as they cook and eat foods from their own and each other's cultural backgrounds.

■ Cooking is language when children "read" recipe cards and charts in sequential order; dictate their own recipes or experiences; share books about foods and cooking; learn new words to name and describe ingredients and actions; and discuss their opinions about recipe procedures and various food favorites.

■ Cooking is creativity when children experience the feeling of combining various elements, make their own choices, compare colors and shapes, and arrange foods and table settings in their own ways.

■ Cooking is even more — a special feeling that happens when a group makes something together. It's a cozy sense of "family" when you share the soup you've made together on a cold, rainy day; it's excitement when you prepare a spring picnic and sit in the grass together to enjoy it — these are moments adults and children can cherish. When you cook with children, you not only make food, you make memories.

COOKING:
AN INTEGRATED EXPERIENCE

Cooking is a hands-, eyes-, nose-, mouth-, ears-, and minds-on activity, in which children experience and talk about every aspect of the process of preparing food. It might mean baking scones, cutting and mixing salad, designing pretzel shapes, or even thoughtfully tasting and comparing different foods.

In a preschool or family day-care setting, natural opportunities to cook arise throughout the day. Children might help fix their own snacks or lunches, or a few children might help prepare meals for the larger group. In addition, you can introduce cooking projects based on children's interests and needs.

HOW IS COOKING A CHILD-INITIATED EXPERIENCE?

To be truly motivating, interesting, and appropriate, a cooking activity needs to come from children's first-hand experiences. Curiosity might arise when someone brings in a special food that children want to know more about, or when the group becomes interested in food-related books checked out from the library. Children may ask questions about how a certain food they eat is grown or prepared, or you all may want to find out more about the culture of a child in the group, including what spe-

Photo: James Levin

cial foods he or she sometimes eats at home. These and other situations provide cues that it's time to introduce a special cooking activity.

Remember, it's wonderful to include cooking as part of your regular routine. Just be sure the recipes you introduce are relevant to your group's real-life experiences. Also, stay flexible. Supplement your scheduled cooking times with opportunities for children to prepare foods independently.

WHAT'S YOUR ROLE?

Cooking, like many other early childhood activities, is a time for children to investigate, manipulate, question, and seek answers at their own pace and in their own unique styles. Therefore, your job becomes one of facilitator and guide rather than director or leader. You set a safe stage for children to investigate interests.

DO let children help choose recipes and locate and gather supplies, as well as participate. Then they'll have opportunities to grow and learn every step of the way.

DO ensure safety and success by setting up well-planned work areas and teaching safe ways to use materials. But take care not to either overprotect or overdirect your group. They will experiment and possibly make a few mistakes, but that's learning, too.

DO be available to assist with difficult tasks, introduce new skills and equipment, and handle hot items. Explain why you're doing this, and avoid taking over. Instead, encourage children to do, practice, and learn.

It's important to keep in mind that when you cook with children, your role will change. In the beginning of your cooking experiences together, you might need to be more involved. But as children become familiar with tools, ingredients, techniques, safety rules, and cleanup guidelines, they will require less intervention from you.

Making Cooking Part of Your Curriculum

INTEGRATE AREAS

As you know, children learn through different media. With this in mind, set up food-related activities in many curriculum areas. Offer children opportunities to investigate cooking in the following areas:

■ *Art area* — Include play clay, cookie cutters, rolling pins, and baking sheets for independent play. Also set out materials for children to make food picture collages, place mats, papier-mâché foods, etc.

■ *Dramatic-play area* — Offer many props such as pots and pans; baking sheets; utensils; empty flour sacks; egg, milk, and cereal cartons; spice containers; aprons; etc.

■ *Library corner* — Fill your bookshelves with selections about baking, foods, and the people who make and eat them around the world.

■ *Music and movement area* — Make up and sing songs and finger plays about your cooking, baking, and cleaning-up activities.

■ *Science area* — Involve children in various experiences that encourage them to see, touch, smell, taste, mix, and combine ingredients, such as smelling some cinnamon and then smelling some nutmeg. Combine the two. What happens to the smell? Do the colors change? What about the texture if you add a little water?

EMPHASIZE SELECTED CONCEPTS OR SKILLS

Children can learn so much just by participating in cooking activities. However, you can give shape to their learning by highlighting particular concepts and skills. For example, chopping

AGES & STAGES

Observe your children to determine their abilities. Then use these guidelines to plan cooking activities that foster growth in each child. Remember, age categories are general. Each child is an individual growing and developing at his or her own pace.

TWO-YEAR-OLDS :

■ need to explore foods with all their senses. Provide extra foods to taste, touch, and smell.

■ like to experience immediate cause and effect. Choose recipes with noticeable changes in food textures, colors, and forms.

■ have short attention spans. Plan quick "instant" recipes.

■ are developing eye-hand coordination. Let children practice pouring into large openings.

■ are active. Don't expect everyone to sit at once.

■ learn by imitation. Model appropriate behaviors.

■ love to say "no." Accept refusals to eat and/or participate in preparation.

■ can be afraid of anything new. Provide lots of opportunities to cook. Most children will join in eventually.

■ need freedom to explore, *with* safety limits. Set up a "do-touch," child-safe environment.

THREE-YEAR-OLDS :

■ like to do things by themselves. Try individual cup/portion recipes.

fruit becomes a language game when, together, you think of as many words as possible to describe the fresh pineapple you're cutting up.

Many adults also find cooking particularly useful in providing math and science experiences that give children natural, real-life opportunities to practice important skills. When children cook, they are involved in the following math skills:

■ *Measuring* — Spooning out one cup of flour and then scooping out one teaspoon of salt to make pancakes helps children take part in and "see" the concepts of *more* and *less*.

■ *Counting* — When children look on a recipe chart or card for a specific number of spoons or banana slices, these numbers have meaning to them.

■ *Sorting* — During cooking experiences, children will sometimes need to sort foods according to color or into groupings of dairy, grain, fruits and vegetables, and meat and beans. Use these efforts when you talk about nutrition.

■ *Graphing* — Cooking provides numerous opportunities to talk about and graph a favorite flavor of fruit shake or least favorite nut butter.

■ *Matching* — You've finished your muffins and they're baking away. Cleaning up means matching utensils to

silhouetted shapes on a pegboard.

At the same time, children are also involved in the following science process skills:

■ *Observing* — Together you might watch as a grape dries to become a raisin, or sun tea changes clear cool water to a liquid that is warm and dark.

■ *Comparing* — Butternut and acorn are both kinds of squash. Children can use their hands and eyes to find differences and similarities.

■ *Predicting* — Before you cook, talk about possible changes, such as how adding extra cinnamon will affect the taste of a fruit crisp; or how freezing will change the appearance of apple juice.

■ *Recording* — Take time to encourage children to use words, pictures, and/or photographs to record your observations of the parsley you planted as it grows.

■ *Investigating* — Just what are all those different "powders" you're using when you make your favorite muffin recipe?

■ *Experimenting* — Which tools get the job done best? Experiment to decide which tool beats eggs the fastest.

Photo: James Levin

Successful Cooking Step by Step

CHOOSING A RECIPE

Selecting a recipe is the first step in planning to cook with children. Consider the following when looking for just the right one:

■ First, evaluate your group's developmental levels and abilities. Consider attention spans, eye-hand coordination, and independence levels. Ask:

• Can the recipe be broken down into a few easy steps?

• Do the processes involve hands-on manipulation of materials and ingredients?

• Can children safely do most of the steps by themselves?

■ Consider your group's individual "personality." Ask:

• Does the recipe relate to children's current interests?

• Does it promote concepts and skills appropriate to my children's developmental levels?

• If foods from other cultures are involved, are they cultures with which my group has had direct experiences?

■ Think about ingredients and materials. Ask:

• Are ingredients easy to find and inexpensive?

• Are they nutritious with very little or no sugar?

• Is it possible that the ingredients are too spicy?

• Are the necessary appliances available?

INTRODUCING THE ACTIVITY

Sharing recipes beforehand lets your children know what to expect during a cooking activity. It also ensures that language is part of their experience. There are several appropriate methods for introducing recipes to preschoolers.

Recipe charts are made in advance with children. First, read the selected recipe aloud. Then, together, break the recipe down into steps, and sequentially illustrate each one in its own box on the chart. You can then print instructions in words and number each box. (See page 16, "Fruit Shakes," for an example.)

You can use recipe charts several times during a cooking activity. First, re-read the chart with children before you begin cooking to get a feel for the flow of the recipe. Then display the chart on a wall or easel to refer to during the actual cooking experience. (Some teachers leave the chart up afterward to help children review the cooking process.) You might also hang used recipe charts in your dramatic-play area so children can pretend to make the same recipes over and over again.

Recipe cards are usually made beforehand by adults. They are similar to charts, except that each step is illustrated on a separate card (usually about the size of a large index card). The size makes them suitable for use with small groups, and also enables greater independence in cooking. (See page 17, "Peanut Butter and Fruit Spread Sandwich.")

Read your recipe cards together before cooking to review the sequence. Then refer to one card at a time as you perform each cooking step.

When making cards, print large, clear letters. Try to copy names of ingredients exactly as they appear on their containers or on packaging labels, so children can identify them. Keep each step extremely simple and illustrate it clearly. For example, if the step calls for children to measure an ingredient, trace the appropriate-sized measuring spoon right onto the card. This way children will be able to match it to the proper spoon.

You might find it helpful to make a cover card for each recipe and list needed ingredients and materials on the back. It's also a good idea to write the recipe name on each card, in case one is misplaced. Laminate the cards for dura- *(continued on page 14)*

■ want to be physically occupied. Use recipes that call for kneading, rolling, stirring, pounding, and/or grating.

■ are developing fine-motor skills. Provide practice in pouring, stirring, chopping, and measuring.

■ need to explore ingredients and materials. Introduce new utensils and foods that allow independent investigation.

■ are becoming more social. Choose recipes in which children can cooperate and share.

FOUR-YEAR-OLDS:

■ are developing sequencing skills. Use recipe cards.

■ can learn about opposites. Talk about "hot" and "cold," "wet" and "dry," "sweet" and "sour," etc.

■ like responsibilities. Make job lists.

■ also experience growth in self-esteem by feeling capable. Foster independence in cooking.

■ are becoming aware of their community. Introduce food related to people and places they know.

■ are beginning to understand time. Use timers.

■ can begin to learn about parts and wholes. Cut foods into halves and quarters.

FIVE-YEAR-OLDS:

■ can learn about food shapes.

■ enjoy using measuring and weighing devices.

■ are able to keep graphs and charts.

■ like to talk about where foods come from.

■ are beginning to understand how bodies use food.

■ like to dictate their own recipes.

(continued on page 14)

NUTRITION NOTES

Whether you plan simple snacks and beverages a few times a week or three full meals every day, you have an effect on children's food choices. Make this effort a positive influence by modeling healthy eating — and feeling healthy as a result. Consider following these suggestions issued in *Dietary Guidelines for Americans*, United States Department of Agriculture and Department of Health and Human Services, 1990.

■ Eat a variety of foods.

■ Maintain a healthy weight through diet and exercise.

■ Choose foods low in fat and cholesterol.

■ Choose a diet high in vegetables, fruits, and whole grains.

■ Use sugar in moderation.

■ Keep alcohol consumption to a minimum.

■ Take time to learn more about nutrition and to offer nutritious food choices to the children in your care.

To find out more, you can talk to a professional nutrition consultant or read some of the many excellent books on the subject, such as those listed below. Also check out the nutrition education materials (for adults and children) at your local public library, college libraries, public schools, and your state or county Cooperative Extension Services. Consider trying the Food and Nutrition Information Center (FNIC), which has a National Agricultural Library where early childhood educators can borrow nutrition materials at no charge. Write: FNIC, National Agricultural Library, Room 304, Beltsville, MD 20705; or call (301) 504-5719 for a list of available resources.

SWEET NOTHINGS

Many health experts, parents, and caregivers agree that children become more active after eating sugary foods. Some attribute this behavior change to the active, stimulating environments where children often receive treats. Still others think there might be a connection between large doses of sugar and chemical changes in the body that can lead to hyperactivity. Everyone agrees that sugary foods can cause tooth decay and have an excess of calories that have little or no nutritional value. Whatever your reasons, it is a good idea to limit sugar in children's daily food choices. Try the following ways to cut down:

■ Choose recipes with little or no sugar, honey, or molasses.

■ If a recipe calls for sugar, experiment with cutting the amount in half.

■ When baking, try substituting apple juice concentrate for sugar.

■ Substitute spreadable fruit for jelly, fillings, and toppings.

■ Use a little cinnamon to sweeten cereal.

■ Rather than serving packaged foods, make your own snacks so you can limit the amount of sugar.

■ Serve fresh fruits and vegetables.

■ Buy 100% fruit juices.

■ Check labels of all packaged foods and choose low-sugar items.

■ Ask parents to send healthy snacks for celebrations, such as frozen fruit pops and muffins instead of ice cream and cake.

■ Set a no-candy rule for your group.

THE CHILD AND ADULT CARE FOOD PROGRAM

The Child and Adult Care Food Program (CACFP) is a division of the United States Department of Agriculture's Food and Nutrition Service. Its purpose is to help children and adult day-care providers in nonprofit and family day-care centers supply nutritionally balanced meals. CACFP provides ongoing training in all aspects of feeding, meal planning, and nutrition information, and even reimburses providers for part of the cost of meals. Although only non-profit programs or family day-care providers can seek help and support from the CACFP, any program can benefit from the knowledge this agency has compiled about early childhood and nutrition. The guidelines developed by the CACFP state that **every child, every day,** should have:

	1-3 years old	3-6 years old
1. Milk		
snack:	1/2 cup	1/2 cup
breakfast:	1/2 cup	3/4 cup
lunch or supper:	1/2 cup	3/4 cup
2. Vegetable, fruit, or full-strength juice		
snack:	1/2 cup	1/2 cup
breakfast:	1/4 cup	1/2 cup
lunch or supper: (2 or more kinds)	1/4 cup	1/2 cup
3. Bread or bread alternatives		
snack:		
Bread	1/2 slice	1/2 slice
roll, muffin, or biscuit	1/2 serving	1/2 serving
cold cereal	1/4 cup	1/3 cup
cooked cereal	1/4 cup	1/4 cup
breakfast:		
Bread	1/2 slice	1/2 slice
roll, muffin, or biscuit	1/2 serving	1/2 serving
cold cereal	1/4 cup	1/3 cup
cooked cereal or pasta	1/4 cup	1/4 cup

	1-3 years old	3-6 years old
lunch or supper:		
Bread	1/2 slice	1/2 slice
roll, muffin, or biscuit	1/2 serving	1/2 serving
cooked cereal or pasta	1/4 cup	1/4 cup
4. Meat or meat alternatives		
snack:		
Lean meat, fish, poultry, or cheese	1/2 oz.	1/2 oz.
egg	1/2	1/2
beans or peas	1/8 cup	1/8 cup
peanut butter	1 tbs.	1 tbs.
nuts or seeds	1/2 oz.	1/2 oz.
yogurt	1/4 cup	1/4 cup
lunch or supper:		
Lean meat, fish, poultry, or cheese	1 oz.	1 1/2 oz.
egg	1	1
beans or peas	1/4 cup	3/8 cup
peanut butter	2 tbs.	3 tbs.
nuts or seeds	1/2 oz.	3/4 oz.

or an equivalent quantity of any combination of the above meat/meat alternatives.

For more information, contact Samuel P. Bauer, Director of Child Nutrition at the Child and Adult Care Food Program, USDA, 3101 Park Center Dr., Rm. 517, Alexandria, VA 22302.

EXCELLENT NUTRITION RESOURCES

■ *Creative Food Experiences for Children* by Mary T. Goodwin and Gerry Pollen (Center for Science in the Public Interest)

■ "Feeding Your Preschooler" poster by Nutrition Graphics, 610 SE Chester, P.O. Box 1527, Corvallis, OR 97339

■ "Food Before Six" pamphlet by the National Dairy Council, 6300 N. River Rd., Rosemont, IL 60018

■ "Food for the Preschooler" pamphlets distributed by the Department of Social Services and Health Services, Health Education, Mailstop LB-12C, Olympia, WA 98504

■ *Meals Without Squeals: Child Care Feeding Guide & Cookbook* by Christine Berman & Jacki Fromer (Bull Publishing)

■ *Nutrition and All That Jazz* by Madalaine Pugliese; available free from the FNIC

■ "Nutrition Education for Preschoolers" USDA Food and Nutrition booklet #FNS-241; available through U.S. Printing Office.

bility, then bind them together with a clip or metal ring. Some programs find it convenient to put recipe cards, materials, and ingredients that will not spoil all in one box.

Sequential instruction cards allow children to complete simple, no-cook recipes by themselves. They are most often used to make individual portion recipes, such as one sandwich or one cup-sized yogurt sundae. They allow you to foster ultimate independence.

Be sure to choose a recipe that has no more than three or four steps and that children can do alone safely. Break down the recipe into individual portions. Then make the sequential instruction cards similarly to the way you make recipe cards — writing and illustrating the steps. Put the cards out on a table in left-to-right progression, each one next to the materials and ingredients children will need to perform that step. After some initial assistance from you, children will be able to move from card to card and eventually complete the entire recipe independently.

USING THE STATION METHOD

Cooking is the kind of activity that often attracts many children and lots of excitement. The "station" method for setting up allows everyone who's interested to participate, yet keeps groups small for safety and educational reasons.

In this method, set up several workstations and let children choose to work in one at a time. Here are tips to keep in mind during preplanning stages:

■ Arrange for extra adult supervision.

■ Plan some stations where children can work independently.

■ Decide where in the room children can play if they opt not to participate at any station.

■ Make sure you have a low work space at each station.

■ Organize movement from station to station by posting a sign-up sheet at each one. Let children know they can move when they see an available chair, or set timers and move from station to station in small groups.

■ Make sure you gather everyone together to review the recipe in its entirety before you begin. Also, discuss how each station operates. Talk about what will be going on where, how many children can work at a station at one time, and when children may move.

Most cooking projects can be done with four stations.

CULTURAL CONSIDERATIONS

Cooking is a natural and fun way to bring children's cultures into your program. Here are suggestions for appropriate ways.

■ **Involve family members.** Preschoolers are not ready to learn about cultures with which they have no firsthand experience. For this reason, be sure to cook foods that reflect the heritages of children in your program. Invite family members to share recipes, customs, and rituals. Ask parents, grandparents, and other family members to make suggestions for dishes to add to your menu.

■ **Make culturally diverse cooking a consistent part of your program.** Plan everyday meals and snacks, not just "special occasion" meals, that include foods from many cultures. Compile a cookbook of children's favorite foods with recipes and keep adding to it as children discover new foods they love.

■ **Avoid stereotyping.** If you do decide to share specific ethnic foods on special holidays, be careful that you're not fostering stereotypes. For example, if Carlito's family brings a Mexican meal for a Cinco de Mayo celebration, be sure to ask Carlito to talk about other foods his family likes to eat during the year. (His choices most probably will include foods familiar to all children in your group as well as foods specific to this family's culture.) Also keep in mind that families of the

The Preparation Station

Set up this space for food preparation. Here children might peel, cut, and prepare fruits and vegetables and measure and mix ingredients following recipe cards. Encourage children to use their senses to touch, taste, and smell.

The Cooking or Heating Station

It's important to set up a separate cooking area so you can have close control over safety. Of course, an adult must always be present. Set this station close to a wall outlet and include pot holders and appliances that are needed, such as a hot plate, toaster oven, electric fry pan, toaster, waffle iron, wok, or other heating device needed to complete your recipe. (If your recipe calls for an adult-sized oven, make sure that it is not a part of this station. It is much too dangerous for young children to use these large, made-for-adult appliances.)

Teach children how to use heating devices safely, supervising at all times, yet giving children some autonomy. For example, children might take turns stirring soup on a hot plate once you have made sure there is no danger of tipping or of children getting burned. Also include egg timers and sand timers at this station that children can set to monitor cooking.

The Cleanup or Dishwashing Station

After an initial introduction, this station may not need adult supervision. Put out a drain board, sponges, paper towels, and drying rags for children to wash, rinse, dry, and put away work materials. Children involved at this station can also be responsible for washing work surfaces before and after cooking, and sweeping and washing floors. Many children enjoy working at this station because, as they clean up after themselves, they feel proud about accomplishing real work independently!

The Table-Setting and Eating Station

This is a great place to incorporate creative imaginations into a cooking experience. Children might make their own place mats, centerpieces, napkin holders, picture menus, and decorative napkins. Groups can practice math as they set a beautiful table, matching the same number of plates and napkins. Then when it's time to eat, children at this station can use trays, aprons, picture menus, order pads, and pencils to serve others!

---

same ethnic background may not eat the same foods or celebrate occasions in the same ways.

■ **Familiarize yourself with special diets.** Some cultures and religions have food requirements. Make sure you know if these pertain to any of the children in your group, and, when possible, consider incorporating these restrictions into your group menus so children don't feel singled out. If you must serve a child a meal that is different from what other children are eating, discuss the reasons with the group. Perhaps the child would like to bring in a taste of his or her food for all to share.

■ **Share recipes and cultures with families.** To continue the spirit of multiculturalism at home, prepare ethnic recipes and send home a sample of a food children have prepared and eaten together. Attach the recipe and a note saying something like this: "We are fortunate to have a beautiful mosaic of children in our program, and we often try to make foods from families' cultures. These are Nori-Maki rolls made from rice and seaweed. Susan's grandmother supplied the recipe, which she brought with her from Japan. Many preschoolers in our group enjoyed them — we hope you do, too!"

■ **Buy unfamiliar foods and experiment.** Every so often, bring in a spice, dessert, fruit, or vegetable that is foreign to you and your group. Investigate it. Taste it. This may help children be more open to new food experiences. Emphasize that while it's okay not to like a particular food, it's not okay to make fun of it.

■ **Remind children of similarities as well as differences.** Families of all cultures, everywhere in the world, use food to nourish their bodies and mark special occasions. Remember that enjoying food together nourishes the mind and the soul!

To create recipe charts with children, list all the materials and ingredients you'll need. Then break down the recipe into simple steps. Write out the steps clearly and number them. Invite children to add pictures to help them follow the chart. Talk about which jobs are for children and which are only for adults.

Fruit Shakes

We need:

a blender

6 plastic knives

a measuring cup

a set of measuring spoons

6 plastic spoons

6 paper cups

1 cup fruit — or

2 cups plain yogurt

1 can frozen apple juice concentrate

1. Cut fruit into small pieces

2. Place chopped fruit, yogurt, and juice concentrate into blender

3. Whip the mixture on high speed until smooth

4. Pour into cups and eat with a spoon

Serves 6 children

Make your recipe cards in advance. First divide the recipe, then write each step on a separate card. Print very clearly, using words and adding pictures. Recipes illustrated in this way can be simple enough for children to complete independently, or more complex for group experiences.

Peanut Butter
and
Fruit
Spread
Sandwich

1. Spread peanut butter on one slice of bread

2. Spread all-fruit on another slice of bread

3. Put the slices together

Cut in half

Eat

SAFETY BY AGE

As you make an effort to constantly consider your children's safety when cooking, keep the following guidelines in mind:

Two- to three-year-olds can safely:
- stir with a spoon
- shake ingredients in a plastic container with a tight cover
- use a butter knife to spread soft butter, jelly, cream cheese, or peanut butter
- mash boiled fruits and vegetables after they have cooled
- combine ingredients in a large bowl and use hands to mix
- make no-cook recipes such as sandwiches and salads
- practice using whisks, spatulas, strainers, colanders, wooden spoons, cookie cutters, and rolling pins.

Three- to four-year-olds can safely do all of the above plus:
- use plastic measuring spoons and cups marked to the proper amounts
- cut soft fruits and boiled vegetables with plastic knives
- combine dry and wet ingredients using forks, whisks, spoons, or rotary beaters
- pour liquids into containers with large openings such as colanders, blenders, or wide-mouth bowls
- use non-electric food grinders, choppers, or juicers.

Four- to five-year-olds can safely do all of the above plus:
- use a heat source placed on a low surface *with adult supervision*
- use a hand mixer *with adult supervision*
- cut flat ingredients with plastic serrated knives, *under adult supervision*
- be taught to use vegetable peelers, cheese graters, and nut crackers.

With all preschoolers, remember to:
- Make sure you have adequate adult supervision, both for children involved in the cooking/cleanup process and for children who are playing elsewhere.
- Make sure all cooking equipment is unbreakable.
- Check the floor area, especially the table where children are washing and rinsing dishes and utensils, to make sure it doesn't get slippery.
- Use electrical appliances with care. Set fry pans, blenders, hot plates, and waffle irons safely out of children's reach. Be sure children are seated and aware of possible dangers. Unplug when not in use.
- Have only adults use ovens and stoves.
- Be firm about asking children to sit when they use knives, peelers, graters, or other sharp utensils, and when the oven is open.
- Hold the pan yourself. Older preschoolers can remove items from pans using a spatula, but remind them that it is very hot. Have plenty of pot holders and/or trivets on hand.

BEWARE OF CHOKING

Preschool-aged children do not have the chewing skills necessary to break down many foods. To significantly reduce the possibility of a child choking:
- **Sit with children while they are eating.**
- **Insist that children remain seated while eating.**
- **Set a calm eating atmosphere.**
- **Prepare certain foods with care:**
  Chop nuts and seeds.
  Slice grapes lengthwise.
  Shred raw vegetables (for children under four).
  Remove inner skins from oranges.
  Remove pits from all fruits.
  Spread peanut butter thinly.
  Serve only tender, boneless meats and fish.
- **Never give popcorn or hard candies to children under four.**

WHAT TO DO IN A CHOKING EMERGENCY

When a child is gasping for breath or not breathing at all, is not able to talk or cry, and his or her face is turning from bright red to blue, you have an emergency that calls for immediate first aid. While another staff member calls 911 or your local emergency number, follow these instructions for the Heimlich Maneuver.

Children Younger Than One Year

1. Place the infant stomach- and face-down on your forearm in a head-down position. Make sure that you hold the head and neck firmly. Rest your forearm against your body for additional support. (For a large infant, lay the baby face-down over your lap, with the head lower than the trunk and firmly supported.)

2. With the heel of your other hand, strike the child rapidly four times between the shoulder blades.

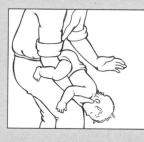

3. If the infant is still not breathing, place the child on his or her back, resting on a hard surface. Put two fingers on the chest, between the nipples, and press rapidly four times.

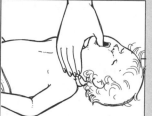

4. If there is no sign of breathing, tip the child's neck slightly and open his mouth. If you see the object that is choking the child, carefully sweep your index finger across the back of the throat to pull it out.

(**NOTE:** Danger of choking can be minimized if children's heads are elevated while they bottle- or breast-feed.)

Children Older Than One Year

1. Place yourself behind the child, on one knee. Speak reassuringly — he or she is probably frightened and tense. Locate the navel with one finger. This will help you position your hands effectively.

2. Place the other hand above the navel, under the rib cage. Make a fist, with your thumb knuckle poking inward.

3. Remove your finger from the navel and place that hand over your fist.

4. Press the child's body against yours and swiftly jerk upward and inward several times. These thrusts can force air upward from the lungs with enough pressure to expel the object caught in the child's throat.

NOTE: If the child still doesn't start to breathe normally, move in front of him and gently open his mouth. Place your thumb over his tongue and your fingers around the lower jaw. If you see the obstruction, try to remove it with a finger sweep.

Do not — under any circumstances — hit the child on the back or reach deep into his throat to pull out the obstruction. If the child coughs up the object into his mouth, hold his head and chin steady and remove it carefully. Be sure not to push the object back down the throat.

Editor's Note: Familiarize yourself and other staff members with first-aid procedures for choking. Seek out an approved first-aid course sponsored by the American Heart Association or the American Red Cross. For more information on first-aid courses, write the American Academy of Pediatrics, 141 Northwest Point Blvd., P.O. Box 927, Elk Grove Village, IL 60009, or call (800) 433-9016. For more information on preventing choking, consult *Caring for Your Baby and Young Child: Birth to Age 5*, by the AAP, Steven B. Shelov, M.D., F.A.A.P., editor in chief (Bantam Books).

Illustrations: Susan Gray

COOKING WITH MIXED-AGE GROUPS

by Kathie Spitzley

Take advantage of your family day-care setting, with its readily available kitchen, to make cooking an integral part of your children's day. Start out simple, with things children can do for themselves or with the assistance of an older child. For example, all children can help fix lunch by rolling chicken in crumbs, placing fish sticks on a tray, or filling small bowls with applesauce. Children two years and older can begin to cut bananas, apples, or other fruits or vegetables (*with plastic knives*) to help make a salad, or halve slices of bread for sandwiches.

Try whole snacks next. Invite children to use a plastic knife, butter spreader, or spoon to spread peanut butter on mini rice cakes. Then add a banana slice, and cover with another rice cake for a snack sandwich! Also plan lunches children can fix themselves. Pita-bread sandwiches, tacos, and individual pizzas are great favorites. Set out all the ingredients children will need. You or older children can help younger ones assemble their selected fillings (meat, crumbled cheese, vegetables, tuna, etc.) into pita bread or taco shells. Everyone can arrange toppings on individual pizzas, but younger children might need help spreading the sauce. (See page 47 for a pizza recipe.)

Consider identifying one day a week as "make lunch" day! Many children will look forward to these days as they become accustomed to helping plan, purchase, and prepare their meals. For a special lunch treat, hold a picnic, even if you all just sit on your front porch. Ask children to choose, prepare, and bag their own food selections.

After making their own snacks and lunches, children can participate in almost any recipe. Here are some tips for safe, successful cooking experiences with mixed-age groups.

■ **Always give cooking projects your complete attention.** When using cutting utensils, limit groups to two or three children. Offer other children alternate cooking tasks while they wait for a turn.

■ **Always bring materials to children's level.** Never let children drag chairs to the stove to stir, taste, or peek at food.

■ **Pre-cut fruits and vegetables into thin strips.** This will help to support children's early attempts at cutting.

■ **Allow children to hold plastic serrated knives only when they have something to cut.** As soon as any child finishes cutting, remove the knife or offer additional materials.

■ **Keep sharp objects out of sight, as well as out of reach, of toddlers.**

■ **Draw recipe cards of your favorite things to make.** If possible, incorporate the colors and designs of your bowls to help children "read" the cards.

■ **Gather materials and ingredients in advance.** Keep them handy so children won't have to wait unnecessarily. When preparing food, let youngest children go first.

■ **If your recipe calls for measuring, invite older children to help you in advance.** Very young children may not be ready to measure.

■ **To avoid egg shells in your finished product, ask children to break eggs into a separate bowl first.**

■ **Include family members in your activities.**

Kathie Spitzley, a family day-care provider in Holland, Michigan, for 10 years, is accredited by the National Association of Family Day Care.

MANAGING COOKING EXPERIENCES

THE VALUE OF SMALL GROUPS

"It's my turn!" "Let me try!" "I can't see!" "Move over!" If you've ever heard these comments from children, you know the value of working in small groups. Children need time and space to explore and interact with each other and materials. If there are too many people, chances are most will be watching while few are doing. Three-, four-, and five-year-olds generally aren't the best at waiting, and they learn very little this way. As you know, children need to be actively involved to absorb and process information.

Of course, cooking experiences are no exception. Four or five children make a good-sized group. Where are the rest of the children? They can be involved in other aspects of the process, such as setting a table, cleaning up, or playing at an unrelated activity. What if more than five children want to cook? Depending on the recipe, you can make several "batches" with different groups, repeat the same activity another day, or just make sure children who didn't participate get a chance next time.

WORKING WITH VOLUNTEERS

To be able to work with children in small groups, you'll probably need to look outside your program for adult volunteers. *(continued on page 24)*

ENCOURAGING COOKING WITH
SPECIAL-NEEDS CHILDREN

Cooking activities invite young children to work together and provide great motivation to use language and social skills. Children also gain practice in motor and cognitive abilities. For a variety of reasons, children with disabilities may have trouble joining in. There are many ways you can help. As you do, remember that because each child has his or her own needs and strengths, it's important to seek advice on adapting activities from therapists and parents. Here are general strategies you can use.

■ *Include tasks at the child's ability level.* Suggest activities that will foster feelings of success. If a child with special needs finds using measuring spoons frustrating, perhaps she could stir ingredients with a wooden spoon.

■ *Offer reachable challenges.* At the same time you provide opportunities for success, encourage the child to try new tasks. Give partial assistance if needed, and praise all attempts at independence.

■ *Promote working together.* A child with special needs may need encouragement to talk, share, and cooperate with others. "Assign" tasks that foster interaction — if the group is making muffins, ask the child to take turns spooning batter into tins.

■ *Help children interact.* Some children with disabilities may not use appropriate facial or body expressions, or may not respond when others talk to them. If necessary, remind a child to smile, look at others, respond, and use social terms such as, "May I have a turn?"

■ *Remind others to include the child with special needs.* Help other children understand what the child can do alone and what she needs help doing. For example, you could say, "Mico, show Noel where the pitcher is. Then she can pour the milk into the bowl herself."

* *

Children with specific disabilities might also benefit from the following adaptations. Consult a therapist to make sure activities meet individual needs.

■ *Children with learning delays* often need more practice in order to master skills than others their age. A repetitive task, such as slicing a banana into small pieces, allows the child to practice and become confident. Language delays may impede children from communicating clearly. Your support and patience will help.

■ *Children with visual disabilities* need extra time to become familiar with materials and procedures. Provide physically stable cookware such as small pitchers with wide bases. To make it easier to keep ingredients in bowls, offer the child ones that are deep rather than shallow. Before you cook, encourage the child to explore utensils freely so he or she can learn about the shape, weight, and size. Show her how to pick up things by their handles. Help the child feel the ingredients and the containers they come in, as you describe and name them. "This baking soda box has flat sides and a flat top, too. The top lifts up on this side. This is where the baking soda comes out." Teach the child to shake the containers (once securely closed) and listen to determine what is inside.

When you explain the activity to the group, ask the child with vision loss to be your assistant. Ask everyone to use language to explain the procedures and labels for materials. Understand that a child with vision loss may have difficulties with position words such as *on* and *behind* and quantity words such as *many* and *few*. As you cook, help the child through the motions. Encourage her to feel the ingredients and discover how they have changed.

■ *Children with hearing loss* may need practice in listening and talking. Make language a necessary part of cooking projects. Provide a limited number of materials and help children ask to share. You could also pair children, making it necessary for them to communicate. Remember, these children may have a difficult time hearing over the noisy conversation that accompanies group cooking. Show others how to get the child's attention by gently tapping his or her shoulder, looking directly at her face, and speaking clearly. Clarify the directions you give by using plenty of gestures, examples, and pictures. Make eye contact frequently.

Cooking is also a good time for a child with hearing loss to increase her vocabulary. New words such as *stir*, *pour*, *roll*, and *pat* have more meaning when the child is actively engaged in these actions. If the child is reluctant to verbalize what she is doing, let her continue working as you describe what is happening.

■ *A child with physical disabilities* may need special adaptations to be able to participate in cooking. A therapist can make suggestions based on the child's particular condition. Some common adaptations to help a child who has trouble grasping include wrapping tape around handles on knives, spoons, and pitchers, or putting bicycle handle grips on straight handles.

Help a child who can't sit independently by providing a standing board he or she can lean against or a chair with a safety belt wrapped securely around it and attached to the table with clamps. If the child is in a wheelchair, make sure the arms of the chair fit under the table so he can reach easily. If needed, place sturdy blocks of wood under the legs to raise the table.

Encourage the child to practice using the utensils before a cooking activity by rolling play clay with a rolling pin, and cutting it with plastic knives. Place measuring cups and spoons, pitchers, scoops, and funnels in the sand or water play table. Show him how to use a hand mixer to create bubbles in soapy water.

■ *Children with behavior disabilities* such as aggression, hyperactivity, or withdrawal can have trouble with the social aspects of cooking. Children who behave aggressively often worry about getting their fair share of materials and time. To help avoid this, organize very small groups, assigning each child his or her own utensils, and making rules of behavior very clear.

A child prone to hyperactive behavior might be able to concentrate only for short periods of time. Watch for signs of restlessness, and suggest a new task or offer choices. When the child does seem involved, encourage sticking with it.

A child who seems withdrawn — hesitating to join in — may need to watch for a while. Or he might prefer to work alone, but near others. Gradually encourage him to interact with the group. Or ask him to help prepare part of the recipe, such as cutting a vegetable to add to the soup. When he seems interested in joining in, stay nearby at first, then move away gradually.

Information and ideas contributed by Merle Karnes, Ed.D., professor of special education, University of Illinois at Urbana.

Parents, grandparents, and senior citizens are obvious — and often successful — populations you can draw from. These "extra" adults can be very helpful, introducing a favorite recipe, running a cooking station, and/or supervising children who choose to play in other areas.

But remember, not all people who want to be with children are prepared to work appropriately with groups of preschoolers. Help make volunteers' and children's cooking experiences positive by preparing everyone beforehand.

VOLUNTEER ORIENTATIONS

If you have ever worked with volunteers, you know it's very important to talk beforehand about working with young children. A good way to orient a new volunteer is to invite him or her to your program. Ask her to observe what children seem to be capable of and/or comfortable with, as well as how you and other teachers talk to and interact with them. Then follow up observation time with adult-to-adult discussions. Talk about what the volunteer saw and heard, your program's philosophy, and relevant policies and goals. Respond to her questions.

Give yourself some room to think, and decide whether you feel comfortable about this particular volunteer working directly with children. If so, decide together what her role will be. Also, talk about safety and how to handle discipline problems. Take time to introduce her to other staff members, children, and the physical setup of your program.

If either of you feels uncomfortable about her working directly with children, explore other services she can offer. Perhaps she can organize your collection of materials and ingredients, or gather recipes from families.

When you combine the interests and skills of adult volunteers with useful management techniques, small-group cooking activities are not only possible, but productive and fun!

KEEPING COSTS DOWN

It is possible to set up and run a cooking program for young children with very little money. A "real" kitchen is not necessary. You can cook or bake almost anything — and use less energy — on small portable heating units. Try a toaster oven instead of an oven, or a hot plate instead of a stove top. Ask friends and parents to lend or even donate small kitchen appliances they no longer need. You can also make a list of equipment you need for cooking — a toaster oven, a blender, pots, pans, bowls, mixers, etc. Then, if families want to give gifts around holidays, birthdays, or the end of school, you might suggest they get together to donate a piece of cooking equipment.

Basic ingredients can also be donated by families, or purchased in bulk at very low prices. (Store ingredients in sealed, unbreakable containers and use a little at a time.) For some recipes, children might each bring in an ingredient. This works especially well with perishable foods such as fruits or vegetables. If your program receives government funds for food, you can include in your budget ingredients for meals and snacks children make themselves. Other creative cost-cutting ideas include holding a special fund-raiser just for your cooking program, and even asking local stores and restaurants to donate excess (but not leftover) food and equipment.

Once you educate other adults about the importance and joy of early childhood cooking experiences, you'll probably find that they are as willing to work toward obtaining this kind of equipment as they are to donate time and materials for other "educational" supplies.

EATING TOGETHER

As you know, you serve as a role model for children in your care. They look to you to learn which words to say, how to act, and even what choices to make. In this way, children learn a great deal by eating with you.

For instance, when your group sits down together with you to share a family style meal or snack, children feel included and important. As you sit with children, you can also maintain safety by watching for choking or foods that might be too hot. You can model calm, appropriate eating behaviors, sending a message that eating is a time to relax and enjoy one another's company. You can help children serve themselves and choose nutritious foods. (If they see you eating broccoli, they just might, too!) You can talk with children about where foods come from, how different foods grow, and which foods children eat at home. Through informal conversations, you can talk about likes and dislikes, favorite foods — any subject at all! All of these are important experiences that bond you and your children more closely together. And all would be difficult, or perhaps impossible, if you limited your role to someone who serves and monitors, or eats in another place entirely!

KNOWING ABOUT FOOD ALLERGIES

Allergies happen when a person's body overreacts against a substance in the environment that most people can tolerate. When an allergic person comes into contact with that substance (called an allergen), his or her body experiences a special type of inflammation. In the case of food allergies, the inflammation can cause an itchy throat, nausea, vomiting, diarrhea, or skin rashes often called hives. Many foods can cause allergic reactions. The most common in young children are eggs, nuts, chocolate, shellfish, cow's milk, and wheat.

Food allergies are usually simple to deal with in early childhood settings if all adults who cook for and eat with young children know: 1) which children may be allergic; 2) what they are allergic to; and 3) what to do if an allergic reaction occurs. Here are some suggestions.

Before you cook:

■ Check children's health records for any mention of food allergies.

■ Post a chart listing the name of each child with allergies, and the substances to which she is allergic.

■ Ask parents whose children have allergies what to do if their child accidentally ingests a food to which she's allergic. Write out these instructions on your chart.

■ Send home copies of recipes you plan to make. Ask specifically if any child is allergic to a food listed in the recipe. If someone is allergic, you might be able to substitute a different ingredient, or you can choose another recipe.

Remember: Parents may be unaware of a child's allergy if the child has never tasted a particular food at home. If you do notice a child reacting to a food, try to keep her calm and comfortable. Ask another adult to contact her parents and physician.

DON'T FORGET TO WASH YOUR HANDS!

Make and illustrate a chart with your children to help everyone remember the following important steps. Laminate and hang it near your sink.

1. Wet your hands with warm running water.

2. Add soap and rub your hands together to make a soapy lather. (Do this away from running water so the lather doesn't wash off.)

3. Make sure you wash the fronts and backs of hands, in between fingers, and under nails.

4. Count to 10 while washing.

5. Rinse well under warm running water. Turn off the faucet.

6. Dry hands thoroughly.

ENVIRONMENTAL CONCERNS

When you make every effort to economize, conserve, and recycle, you help children learn to do the same.

SAVE WATER
● Don't run water unnecessarily.
● Use a filled dishpan or sink to wash dishes. Rinse them in running water turned on halfway.
● If you have a dishwasher, only run it when it's full.
● Reuse dishwater to water plants — soap is really okay!
● Fix leaky faucets immediately.

SAVE ENERGY
● Keep your refrigerator/freezer at the lowest safe setting.
● Vacuum the back of your refrigerator and defrost your freezer regularly.
● Preheat your oven for the shortest time possible.
● Turn off the lights when you leave an area.

SAVE RESOURCES
● Buy only what you need.
● Choose foods packed in paper instead of plastic.
● Look for the recycled seal on packaging.
● When shopping, bring your own bags or ask for paper bags.
● Grow and eat food from your own garden. Keep a compost heap.
● Recycle!

When cooking and shopping with children, be sure to talk to them about your environmentally conscious choices and actions. Give them opportunities to make decisions about bettering their environment and encourage their environmental efforts. Helping children learn good habits now can help make the world a cleaner, healthier place to live in generations to come!

SETTING UP
FOR COOKING

When you consider your room arrangement, keep in mind that exciting cooking activities for preschoolers can take many forms — some are adult directed, some independent; some require a heat source, others do not. Similarly, successful cooking activities take place in a variety of "kitchen" arrangements. The important thing is to create an environment where children can experience cooking's joys, challenges, and growth opportunities in safe and appropriate ways. Here are some suggestions.

ADOPT A KITCHEN

As you know, many programs have kitchen areas already — institutional kitchens where cooks prepare meals; or, in family day-care homes, family style kitchens. You can easily adapt these facilities for children's use.

First, "child-proof" the room. Cover electrical outlets with safety plugs. Hide and/or secure electrical cords to walls, floors, and cabinets. Add safety catches to all cabinet doors. Place all cleaning solutions and other dangerous materials in one high storage area and lock it. Put all sharp utensils out of children's reach. Last of all, do one more search for other potential hazards.

Next, make the section around the

Photo: James Levin

oven, stove, sink, and refrigerator an "Adults Only" area. Place brightly colored tape on the floor to remind children to enter this area *only* when accompanied by an adult. Make the section just wide enough so children and adults can function safely without taking up too much of the rest of the room. Three feet is often a good size, but, of course, you must decide what works best in your setting.

CREATE YOUR OWN "PORTABLE" KITCHEN

If you don't have kitchen facilities available, make your own. Use a very sturdy commercial or homemade cart with wheels. Arrange all the appliances and utensils you'll need for cooking projects on the cart. Be sure to include small appliances that will substitute for a stove and oven, such as a toaster oven, hot plate, and electric fry pan. Also include basins or a plastic portable sink to serve as makeshift water sources. (You can find portable sinks in early childhood supply catalogs.) Label the cart with words and pictures to describe the contents, then place it in a locked storage area. When your group has the urge to cook, simply wheel the cart out for an instant kitchen!

SET UP WORK AREAS

Any cooking arrangement requires work areas to prepare food. Provide low tables and child-sized chairs so children can sit and work safely and comfortably. In addition to worktables, set up another small table near an outlet. During cooking projects, place electrical appliances such as blenders and toaster ovens on this table. This arrangement keeps appliances away from children's work space, and, at the same time, allows them to see easily when you operate appliances. (Remember, for safety reasons, children should always be seated while they watch.)

SET UP FOR MAXIMUM INDEPENDENCE

As a part of your setup, you'll want to offer children opportunities to prepare food by themselves. This might be a choice during free play, as a make-your-own-snack activity, or as part of the "job" of snack helpers. To do this, you'll need a long, low table so you can set out sequential instruction cards and all the necessary materials in a left-to-right progression. (This kind of activity works best when children have had some experience with cooking. See page 14 for information on sequential instruction cards.)

As you plan your room arrangement to foster children's independence, organize ways children can find, identify, and put away utensils and ingredients. A pegboard is a great place to start! Cut construction paper shapes of the utensils that will hang, such as small fry pans, spatulas, and muffin tins. Laminate or cover the shapes with clear adhesive and tape them to the pegboard, installing a hook above each. Children can easily find the utensils they need, then match them to their cut-out shapes at cleanup.

Use low, open shelves to store materials such as unbreakable mixing bowls and non-perishable foods. Place a picture of each item on the shelf so children can match up while cleaning up. (Keep all foods sealed in unbreakable, see-through containers labeled with pictures and words so children can identify them easily.) Many teachers find it convenient to store small items together in boxes.

Don't forget materials that foster independent cleaning — liquid soap, sponges, a drain board at the sink or water basin, and child-sized brooms, mops, and dustpans nearby.

Of course, any unsafe cooking or cleaning items should be stored in the "Adults Only" section, out of children's reach.

THE TOP THREE SETUP RULES FOR COOKING

However you decide to arrange your room for cooking, remember these three rules.

1.

Keep it simple, supervised, and safe. Your cooking area must be easily accessible to children and easy to supervise; simple for children to use independently and with adult assistance; and safe for children to be in.

2.

Be as organized as possible. When "everything has a place and there's a place for everything," children can use and clean up materials with confidence. And you are able to see at a glance what is available and what might be needed.

3.

Find the right location. Because cooking centers tend to be active, exciting places, try to locate yours in an out-of-the-way area where activities are less likely to be disruptive or disrupted. If at all possible, a sink should be close by for hand washing and cleanup. Plus, remember that spills happen! If the floor in your food preparation area is washable, cleanup will be so much easier.

STOCKING UP

You can begin cooking using only the materials required in the simplest recipes. Then, over time, add to your equipment by gathering, saving, collecting, and purchasing some of the following.

- ▼ Aprons
- ▼ A blender
- ▼ Clear, unbreakable pots and baking pans
- ▼ A colander
- ▼ Cookie sheets and cutters
- ▼ Cutting boards
- ▼ Electric and/or hand mixers
- ▼ An electric fry pan
- ▼ Forks
- ▼ Graters
- ▼ A hot plate
- ▼ A juicer
- ▼ Knives — sharp and plastic
- ▼ Loaf pans
- ▼ Low tables and chairs
- ▼ Measuring cups and spoons
- ▼ A microwave oven
- ▼ Muffin tins
- ▼ Openers for bottles and cans
- ▼ An oven
- ▼ Oven mitts and pot holders
- ▼ A rolling pin
- ▼ A rotary beater
- ▼ Saucepans
- ▼ Spatulas
- ▼ A stove
- ▼ A timer
- ▼ A toaster and toaster-oven
- ▼ Unbreakable mixing bowls
- ▼ Vegetable brushes and peelers
- ▼ A waffle iron
- ▼ Whisks
- ▼ Wooden mixing spoons
- ▼ Plus, cleanup materials, too!

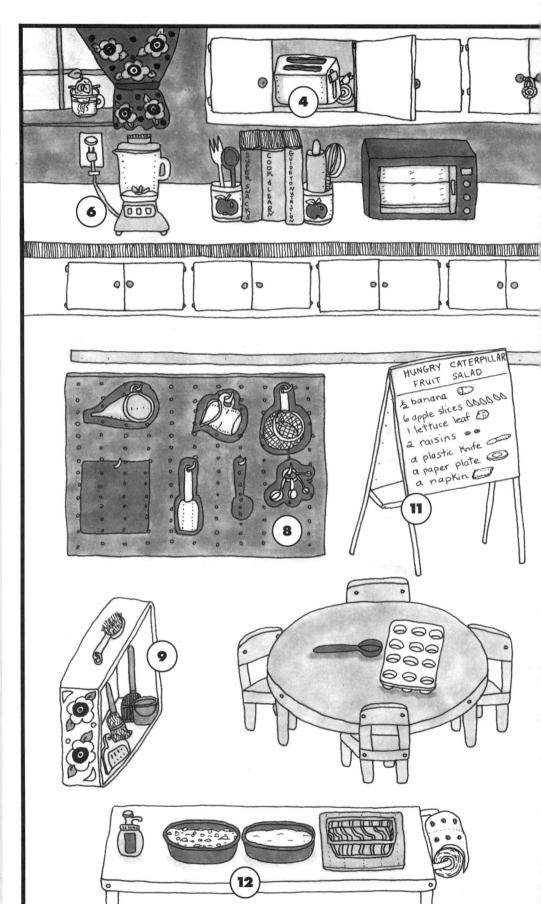

HUNGRY CATERPILLAR
FRUIT SALAD
½ banana
6 apple slices
1 lettuce leaf
2 raisins
a plastic knife
a paper plate
a napkin

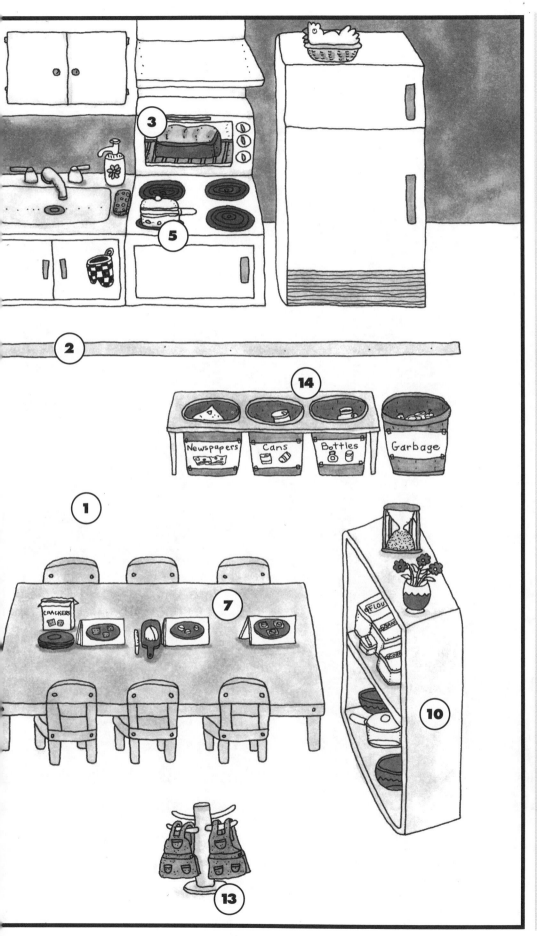

A SUPER SETUP!

With lots of supplies or even just a few, you can create a successful setup for cooking. The numbers below correspond to important elements in the diagram to the left. Use the suggestions offered here and adapt them to your own setting and needs.

1. Choose an area where floors can be washed easily.

2. Use brightly colored tape to set off the "Adult Area." Keep major appliances and items that require adult supervision here.

3. If possible, use an oven with a large window, and a stove with control knobs above children's reach.

4. Store electrical appliances and sharp knives out of children's reach.

5. When possible, use unbreakable, see-through cook- and bakeware to allow children to watch food changes in action.

6. Cover and/or secure electrical cords when using appliances.

7. Provide low, roomy tables that offer plenty of room to work. Set out picture instructions and everything children will need to prepare food independently.

8. Hang utensils within children's reach. Attach paper silhouettes to the pegboard for orderly storage and easy cleanup.

9. Offer child-sized mops, brooms, dustpans, and buckets.

10. Provide low shelves for materials and ingredients. Store ingredients in clear, unbreakable, airtight containers. Label with words and pictures.

11. Hang recipe charts where all chefs can see them.

12. Create a washing station by filling basins with clear and soapy water. Include a drain board, liquid soap, sponges, dish towels, and paper towels.

13. Offer easy-to-reach places to hang aprons.

14. Foster concern about the environment! Set out containers for recycling.

LEARNING AND GROWING

As the chart on the next three pages shows, young children encounter opportunities to develop socially, emotionally, physically, cognitively, and creatively as they cook. In each area of development, cooking activities also enhance or refine key skills or concepts. Feel free to reproduce the chart to help colleagues and parents appreciate the important role cooking can play in developing the whole child.

Here's how to follow the chart: Each entry begins with a description of a skill or concept and how it develops as children cook. Under "Ways to Assist," you'll find suggestions you can use to promote further development in that area. Under "Developmental Considerations" there are guidelines to help you know what to expect from younger children (two/threes) and from older preschoolers (four/fives). Naturally, because behavior varies greatly at all ages, you'll want to view these as guidelines only.

WITH COOKING

SOCIAL & EMOTIONAL DEVELOPMENT

DEVELOPING SELF-CONFIDENCE

Cooking activities enable young children to act independently and use "grown-up" materials to create something they can actually eat. Because the process and product of cooking are both "real," children feel they can truly do something useful. At the same time, they begin to feel competent and trusted, emotions that contribute to self-confidence.

Ways to Assist

■ Help children develop mastery by giving them lots of opportunities to become familiar with cooking materials and procedures. Repeat favorite recipes several times, encouraging children to try more and more tasks independently.

■ Use techniques that allow children to do as much as possible by themselves. Mark measuring cups with tape so they can "measure to the line." When appropriate, pre-cut fruits and vegetables into large pieces to make chopping easier. Keep ingredients in familiar containers so children can learn to recognize them, and can retrieve them for recipes and return them to their places.

Developmental Considerations

■ Two- to three-year-olds like to dive right into cooking with all their senses. Set up simple food preparation activities — arranging cheese and crackers or adding toppings to yogurt — in which they can work independently and be successful.

■ Four- to five-year-olds are capable of preparing more complex recipes. Introduce them to new techniques one at a time, then offer opportunities for practice toward mastery.

COOPERATING & SHARING

When several children prepare a recipe together, they cooperate and share in a real-life situation. They also experience first-hand that individuals can be part of a group, and that working with others can help reach a goal. In this way, young children begin to appreciate the value of cooperation.

Ways to Assist

■ Set up stations where children can choose to work on the tasks that most interest them. Then review how each child contributed to the whole process. "Marcus mixed the ingredients. Manuel helped wash dishes. Jessica and Jerome set a beautiful table. We all worked together to make a lovely lunch!"

■ Help children share foods. When you find you've cooked more than you need, talk with children about people you might share with — a neighbor, another person who works with your group, or someone less fortunate.

Developmental Considerations

■ Two- to three-year-olds probably won't be ready to share yet, and food can be especially difficult. However, children are more likely to share if they feel that their own needs will be met. Help children feel assured by providing samples and offering healthy snacks whenever they are hungry. Don't force.

■ Four- to five-year-olds are often eager to share a creation they made "all by themselves." To enhance these feelings, you might have a discussion about how people feel when they give and receive food.

MULTICULTURAL AWARENESS

Cooking is a good way to help children see cultural similarities and differences in concrete ways. Through activities involving cooking and food, children can see this: "Many of us eat peanut butter and jelly, hamburgers, and cereal, but some of us also eat foods that are special to our backgrounds!"

Ways to Assist

■ Model an attitude that welcomes and celebrates diversity.

■ Help children understand the similarities that underlie the differences they see. When they notice the many different foods people bring for lunch, talk about the fact that many kinds of foods can be healthy and help bodies grow.

■ When cultural meals are shared, be sure to help children realize that this is food people eat sometimes or at special occasions. Avoid stereotyping — grouping people only by a certain kind(s) of food.

■ Explore similarities and variations by choosing one food staple, such as noodles or bread, and finding many different ways to cook and eat it.

Developmental Considerations

■ Two- to three-year-olds aren't ready to understand the cultural aspects of food, but they can begin to develop positive attitudes toward diversity.

■ Four- to five-year-olds are interested and can begin to understand where foods come from and the various ways they can be prepared.

LEARNING AND GROWING

PHYSICAL DEVELOPMENT

FINE- AND GROSS-MOTOR SKILLS

A wonderful by-product of hands-on cooking experiences is that children use their hands! As they manipulate ingredients, they practice and refine control over small hand muscles. Naturally, their developing coordination transfers to other important skills such as cutting with scissors and holding pencils.

Ways to Assist
■ Provide children with many opportunities to use their hands during cooking activities. Emphasize actions as you cook: "Let's make sure we chop this up extra-small!" "Let's roll this dough into little balls."
■ Introduce a variety of non-electric tools that require children to use their hands in different ways — slicing, kneading, turning, etc. Encourage children to experiment with ways to use the tools, as well as with ways to use their hands.

Developmental Considerations
■ Two- to three-year-olds are just developing fine-motor skills. They need lots of practice repeating the same tasks to achieve mastery. Keep your expectations in line with children's abilities, and support their efforts and progress.
■ Four- to five-year-olds can learn to perform more delicate cooking techniques such as cracking eggs. Handle drops and spills as matter-of-factly as possible.

HEALTHY EATING AND NUTRITION

Because young children learn so much from the important adults in their lives and through hands-on participation, the healthy eating habits and fun, nutritious foods you introduce can influence their eating patterns for the rest of their lives.

Ways to Assist
■ When cooking with children, use recipes that exemplify healthy eating, such as those found in the activity plans. At the same time, keep healthy eating fun by making sure the food children cook or bake and the food you serve taste good to children. Offer small tastes of new foods to children who want to explore.
■ Bring parents and family members into your plans for healthy eating by sharing healthy recipes and asking them to contribute recipes from home that typify healthy eating.
■ Serve healthy snacks, keeping sugar at a bare minimum and concentrating on foods that are fresh, include whole grains, and are as free from preservatives as possible.
■ As you cook, serve, and eat together, talk about what makes foods healthy. And because you're such an important role model, make sure the food you eat in front of children is good for you.

Developmental Considerations
■ Two- to three-year-olds are not ready to learn about nutrition but will benefit from hearing you verbally recognize healthy foods and healthy eating patterns.
■ Four- to five-year-olds usually enjoy learning, and discerning, which foods are healthy and which are not.

COGNITIVE DEVELOPMENT

EMERGENT LITERACY

Speaking, listening, reading, writing — the primary skills of language development — are all part of a total cooking experience. When children use recipe cards and charts, they come to know words and pictures as meaningful symbols. Following recipes shows children one way that print can be useful to them. And children practice listening and speaking and learn new vocabulary when the group discusses cooking projects and makes charts and books based on cooking experiences.

Ways to Assist
■ Look for ways to add language components before, during, and after cooking activities. Encourage lots of whole-group and one-to-one discussions about materials, procedures, changes, and other topics of interest to children.
■ Ask open-ended questions to promote creative thinking and language use. Questions are open-ended if they have no right or wrong answers. Phrases such as, "What do you think?" or "How do you feel?" are good ways to begin.

Developmental Considerations
■ Two- to three-year-olds develop vocabulary quickly. Provide them with words to fit their tools and actions. "Suky, it looks like you are having fun *stirring* with that *wooden spoon.*"
■ Four- to five-year-olds crave autonomy. Help them learn to "read" and follow picture recipe cards on their own. Experienced cooks of this age also enjoy inventing and then "writing" their own recipes.

WITH COOKING

SCIENCE PROCESS SKILLS

Cooking invites preschoolers to ask questions, seek responses, and practice science skills as they observe, investigate, and experiment with changes in shape, form, texture, and color. As a result, young children begin to make important discoveries about their world. "When I mix water with flour I get a soft, moist dough. When I cook it, it turns tan and hard ... "

Ways to Assist

■ Offer children plenty of time to mix, combine, and experiment with ingredients. Even if the results sometimes seem less than appetizing to you, children gain valuable scientific experiences and feel proud of their efforts.

■ Provide opportunities for children to predict and compare outcomes. Ask questions such as, "If we add flour to this egg mixture, what do you think will happen?" Then test out your predictions. By using words and pictures to record the experience, you can add another important science and language skill, and help round out the experience.

Developmental Considerations

■ Two- to three-year-olds need to witness simple changes. Try making yogurt shakes in a blender or shaking cream to make butter. Verbalize the changes at the same time.

■ Four- to five-year-olds are ready to learn more about parts of foods and how they are produced or grown. Take field trips to farms, markets, bakeries, factories, or other food producing places.

MATHEMATICAL SKILLS

Preparing and serving food offers children many opportunities to match, sequence, pattern, sort, classify, count, measure, graph, notice shape, and experiment with part-to-whole relationships and one-to-one correspondence. As you know, each of these actions is an important, appropriate math experience for preschoolers.

Ways to Assist

■ Seek out ways to include and highlight math skills as you cook. Make graphs of ingredients or of children's likes and dislikes, and review cooking processes by recalling what you did first, next, and last. Practice dividing fruits and vegetables into enough parts so everyone can have a piece. Classify ingredients into dry or wet, solid or liquid, yummy or yucky; and sort foods by color or shape. Encourage children to match utensils to outlines on recipe cards and notice same- as well as different-shaped foods.

Developmental Considerations

■ Two- to three-year-olds are not ready for more complex processes, such as graphing or sequencing, but they can begin to sort into two simple categories or match two things that are the same. Help children with these processes by verbalizing their actions: "Yes, Lynette, those are all spoons; they match."

■ Four- to five-year-olds can experiment with more difficult math-related tasks and concepts, such as following numbered sequenced recipe cards with more steps.

CREATIVE DEVELOPMENT

MAKING CREATIVE CHOICES

To many adult chefs, cooking is an extremely creative process. Children also feel creative when they are able to make choices as they select, cook, and eat food. Creativity is also an important factor in cooking when children can design their own foods, such as funny-face pancakes or creepy-crawly vegetable salads.

Ways to Assist

■ Seek out recipes that provide opportunities to make individual choices. Then be flexible about optional ingredients. Allow children to pick, choose, and substitute when possible.

■ Ask children to help you invent new ways to jazz up old recipes. They might suggest adding bananas to peanut butter sandwiches, making edible "machines" out of celery and carrot slices, and other ideas you would never have thought of!

■ Offer opportunities for children to decorate foods in inventive but nutritious ways, such as choosing unsweetened coconut, fresh fruits, and unsweetened granola to create a yogurt parfait.

Developmental Considerations

■ Two- to three-year-olds notice color and texture in their environment. Serve foods with an eye toward these features to add an aesthetic component to cooking and eating.

■ Four- to five-year-olds have had more experience with foods and are more familiar with their likes and dislikes. They can have great fun inventing and trying out their own recipes!

TALKING WITH FAMILIES ABOUT COOKING

Cooking is a familiar activity to most families and the family kitchen is often a comfortable spot to enjoy each other's company. However, not every family recognizes cooking as an important growth and learning experience for preschoolers. Many might be reluctant to allow their children to help in the kitchen due to concerns about safety. As an early childhood educator, you can help family members understand that cooking can foster children's self-esteem and confidence, as well as help build important social, creative, and cognitive skills.

Here are ways to present cooking so families can help children experience the joys of learning and working with others.

Invite families to join in the fun.

Many parents, grandparents, and older brothers and sisters certainly know how to cook. Invite these family members in to help. Begin with simple, healthy sandwiches or snacks. Then, as adults and children become more experienced, encourage families to suggest favorite recipes, help you prepare step-by-step recipe cards, and assist children in every phase of preparation. Point out what children are learning as you work together.

Send home recipes.

Every time you cook together, try to save a little food for each child to share with his or her family. Be sure to include the recipe and hints about ways children can help make the food at home.

Make a videotape of a group cooking experience.

If you have access to a video camera, ask someone to come in to tape a cooking experience from start to finish — choosing a recipe, making a list of ingredients, taking a shopping trip, setting up, doing the preparations, and finally enjoying your food together. When the tape is complete, ask other staff members to help you by adding informative narration about how and what children are learning during every step of the process.

Host a special food event.

Invite families to a dinner, lunch, or breakfast that children have helped prepare. Write and decorate invitations together, set tables with place mats and centerpieces children have made, and serve the food together. Display photographs with captions that highlight skills children practiced as they cooked this special meal. You can also share your video!

Share related information.

Copy the letter on the following page to send home with children. Also, send home articles from this book and other sources about safety, nutrition, and related topics that help support your ideas about the importance of cooking with children.

LEARNING THROUGH COOKING:
A MESSAGE TO FAMILIES

Dear Parents,

Throughout the year we often cook together. Many of our children love these times. They work in small groups, with adult supervision, to prepare foods they can really eat and share. We cherish these special cooking moments because children are truly involved with and excited about what they are doing.

We are also aware of the skills and concepts children come to understand more completely. Math skills are enhanced as children measure with spoons and cups, and count and estimate ingredients. Stirring, beating, shaking, rolling, pounding, and kneading all provide small hand muscles the exercise they'll need later for holding pencils. Children also experience sharing and cooperating with others, two important social skills. They mix dry and wet ingredients, and watch foods change properties through exposure to heat and cold — both science concepts. Sometimes older children "read" step-by-step recipe cards, or talk and share books about where foods come from and how they grow, which are great language arts experiences. At the same time, we have the immense joy of watching children beam with pride as they do things all by themselves! When you offer your child these valuable learning experiences at home, remember to take a few safety precautions.

- Hide or secure all electrical cords so children can't pull or chew on them.
- Cover all electric sockets with safety plugs and place safety guards on cabinet drawers and doors.
- Face pot handles toward the center of the stove.
- Work on a low surface or seat your child in a high seat so he or she can see and participate with ease.
- Sit *with* children while using electrical appliances.
- Insist that children sit while cutting.
- Seat children far enough from the stove or oven so they can't reach the hot surface.
- Supervise children's use of hot tap water.
- Never let children use the stove, oven, or garbage disposal. Let them watch from a safe distance.
- **Put all dangerous or poisonous products in one place and out of reach.**

Your child can help by:
- stirring with a spoon, whisk, or fork
- shaking ingredients in a plastic self-seal bag or container with a tight lid
- cutting soft fruits and parboiled vegetables with a butter knife
- spreading butter, cream cheese, peanut butter, etc.
- mashing soft fruits and vegetables
- pouring liquids into and out of spoons, cups, and bowls (Expect some spills!)
- turning a rotary beater
- learning to use a vegetable peeler
- rolling, pounding, cutting, and kneading dough or chopped meat
- cleaning up! Many children love to sweep, use sponges, and wash dishes.

Happy cooking! We'd love to hear about your experiences.

Sincerely,

_____

Teacher

ACTIVITY PLANS

FOR TWOS, THREES, FOURS, AND FIVES

Whole Wheat Scones
1. Wash hands and table top.
2. Measure all ingredients.
3. Sift flour, salt, and baking powder into bowl.
4. Add margarine and mix with hands.
5. Add milk and mix again with hands.
6. Dust tabletop with flour.
7. Roll dough until it's this thick.
8. Spr... shortenin... bakin...
9. Use ... cutters ... circles...
10. P... on ba... eet.
11. B... degre... min...

USING THE
ACTIVITY PLANS

The activity plans on the following pages offer engaging cooking experiences appropriate for two-, three-, four-, and five-year-old children. They will also help you introduce children to, and offer them practice with, many important preschool skills and concepts. Have fun using these plans as cooking interests arise in your group.

GETTING THE MOST FROM THE ACTIVITY PLANS

Because each plan is designed with a specific age in mind, the set together offers help in structuring cooking experiences that are developmentally appropriate to the interests and abilities of twos, threes, fours, and fives. Naturally, these ages represent a wide range of developmental levels, so you may find that certain plans need to be adapted for your particular group. And to truly get the most from the plans, look at all 40 for ideas to simplify, modify, or extend for your children.

The format is simple and easy to follow. Each plan includes most of these sections:

■ **AIM:** The value of the activity is explained through a listing of the key skills and learning concepts children will practice.

■ **GROUP SIZE:** The suggested group size is the optimum number of children to involve at one time. Naturally, you'll adjust this number to meet your own needs.

■ **MATERIALS:** Basic materials — most of which you'll already have in your room — or special items to gather are suggested here.

■ **INGREDIENTS:** Everything you'll need to make the recipe.

■ **IN ADVANCE:** This is an occasional heading found in some plans. It often outlines materials to prepare or arrangements to make before introducing an activity.

■ **GETTING READY:** Here you'll find ways to introduce the theme to one child, a small group, or a large group. Open-ended questions help children think about a topic. Handling props, brainstorming ideas, creating experience charts, and sharing stories are other ways to encourage hands-on participation.

■ **BEGIN:** Look for suggestions to introduce materials, to help children get started, and to guide young cooks through preparing recipes. You'll also find additional suggestions for open-ended questions. And some activities will feature extension ideas to further enhance an experience.

■ **REMEMBER:** This section offers considerations to keep in mind about how children develop and what to expect from different ages. There may also be an occasional safety reminder or a tip on ways to relate other skills and concepts to the activity theme.

■ **BOOKS:** Each plan features at least three carefully chosen books that enhance or extend the delightful experience of cooking together.

SHARING THE PLANS WITH OTHERS

You may duplicate each plan for educational use, so don't hesitate to share! Fellow teachers, aides, and volunteers in your program, as well as family members at home, can all benefit. What's more, you communicate your philosophy of child-centered learning. By offering tips about how to plan and present safe cooking projects, you help other adults understand cooking's rich potential to aid in the development of young bodies, minds, and spirits.

USING THE ACTIVITY INDEX

The index on pages 78-79 lists each activity plan, along with the developmental areas and skills it enhances. Use the index to:

▼ Determine the full range of skills and concepts covered in the plans.

▼ Highlight specific skills or developmental areas a plan reinforces when talking with family members.

▼ Identify and locate an activity that reinforces a particular skill on which you want to focus.

▼ Assist in finding activities that complement your group's present interests.

COOKING

Roll, roll, roll a snack!

SANDWICH LOGS

Aim: Children will use fine-motor skills and be able to make choices as they create a fun snack.

Group Size: Two or three children.

Materials: Balls, toy wheels, cardboard cylinders, and other objects that roll; a few blunt plastic knives and plastic spoons; rolling pins; and paper plates and napkins.

Ingredients: One slice of whole-grain bread per child; and peanut butter, cream cheese, and all-fruit spread to use as toppings.

GETTING READY

Place toy wheels, balls, cylinders, and other objects in a pile. Invite children to play freely with them. As they explore, draw attention to the way the objects move. Explain that this way of moving is called "rolling." Encourage children to experiment. They can try rolling objects across the floor, to other children, and down a slide or ramp.

Then play a movement game. On a clean, soft floor, use your whole body to roll like the objects.

BEGIN

Gather your group to make sandwich logs. Wash your hands together and sit down at your kitchen or snack table. Then offer each child a slice of crustless bread. Bring out the rolling pins and take time to talk again about things that roll. Show children how to use the rolling pins to flatten their bread slices.

Next, bring out small bowls of peanut butter, cream cheese, and all-fruit spread. Invite children to choose which spread or spreads they want to put on their sandwiches. Help them use plastic spoons or knives to spread on small amounts. As they do, verbalize their actions: "Rory, you chose peanut butter and all-fruit for your sandwich. You spread them so smoothly on your bread."

Now demonstrate how to roll up the bread into cylinder shapes. Cut the cylinders in half, and eat your log sandwiches!

Remember

• Be sure children have plenty of rolling room. You may need to step in occasionally to prevent collisions.

• Some children might not like it if their hands feel sticky. Keep damp napkins or cloths available for quick wash-ups.

BOOKS

These books offer other cooking suggestions.	▪ *Gingerbread Tales*, Ed. by David Gamon (AD Bragdon)	▪ *Kindergarten Cooks* by Nellie Edge (Peninsula WA)	▪ *Making Pretzels: Little Chef Series* (Viking Penguin)

COOKING

Have fun when twos make these cooking creations!

FUNNY-FACE PANCAKE SNACK

Aim: Children will experience feelings of accomplishment as they use creative skills to make a delicious snack.

Group Size: Three to six children.

Materials: At least one whole-wheat pancake per child; a mixing bowl and spoon, measuring spoons and cups, a griddle, a ladle, a spatula, and a plate; waxed paper; vanilla yogurt; toppings such as blueberries, raisins, pineapple chunks, and orange slices; cups; water; paper towels; small bowls; plastic spoons; cookie cutters; and all-fruit spread.

Pancake Ingredients: (For six 7-inch pancakes) 1 egg, 1 cup buttermilk, 2 tablespoons vegetable oil, 1 cup whole-wheat flour, a level tablespoon sugar, 1 teaspoon baking powder, 1/2 teaspoon baking soda, and 1/2 teaspoon salt.

GETTING READY

Measure out the ingredients and beat the egg. Explain that you are going to make pancakes for snack. Invite interested children to help.

Show children the ingredients and utensils, and name them together. Then talk about your actions as you pour and mix. When the batter is ready, invite children to stay and watch you cook. (Some may do so; others may move to another activity, supervised by another adult.) Make sure children are well out of the way, then grease and heat the griddle or a hot pan and ladle about 1/4 cup of batter into the center. Cook until bubbles form on top. Turn the pancake with a spatula and brown the other side. As pancakes are finished, place them on a plate and cover each with waxed paper. Refrigerate until cool.

Put fruits and yogurt into bowls. Set the table with a paper towel and small spoon at each place. Place a pancake on each paper towel. Let children know it's time to wash their hands.

BEGIN

Show children the pancakes and say, "Here are the pancakes we mixed and cooked. Everyone has one. Let's use this fruit to make funny faces on our pancakes." Demonstrate one way to make a face. Say, "I'm using two raisins for the eyes. What could I use for a mouth? What a funny face!" Ask children to name the fruits and the parts of their faces as they create. When they finish, put out water or cold milk and enjoy eating your funny-face pancakes together!

Another time, invite children to cut their pancakes using cookie cutters. Decorate the shapes with toppings such as yogurt, fruit pieces, and all-fruit spread. Have fun eating the shapes and the scraps.

Remember

▪ Invite children to help mix but make sure they are nowhere near the hot griddle.

▪ Hands need to be washed thoroughly.

▪ Leave plenty of room for creativity — some children may want to give their faces three noses!

▪ Remind children to take only as much as they can eat; if they are still hungry, they can have more.

▪ Establish a cleanup routine so children get used to wiping their mouths, washing their hands, and disposing of paper towels.

BOOKS

Here are books that give twos a good look at faces.

▪ *Where's Your Nose?* by Laura Rader (Grosset & Dunlap)

▪ *Masks* by Mitsumasa Anno (Putnam Publishing Group)

▪ *My Dressing Book* by Betsey Bober Polivy and Jane Gelbard (Grosset & Dunlap)

COOKING

Use all your senses to create this apple snack!

FIVE-SENSE APPLESAUCE

Aim: Children will use their senses of smell, touch, taste, hearing, and sight as they prepare a nutritious snack.

Group Size: Three or four children.

Materials: Two basins filled halfway with water; vegetable brushes; drying rags; a vegetable peeler and an apple corer/slicer (for adult use); a saucepan; a stovetop or hot plate; wooden spoons; a large bowl; paper cups; plastic spoons; and stickers.

Ingredients: Approximately one dozen large red or green baking apples; and cinnamon and lemon juice (optional).

GETTING READY

Gather children together and pass around apples. Talk about how they feel — smooth and round with stiff, pointy stems. Talk about how they look — red or green and shiny. Talk about their smell — sweet and fresh. Then cut open one apple. Use your senses again to explore the inside.

Next, put out vegetable scrub brushes, drying rags, and a few basins with water. Show children how to wash the apples and place them in a bowl.

Try this chant while you scrub:

> *Two little apples hanging in a tree.*
> *Two little apples smiled down at me.*
> *I shook that tree, hard as I could,*
> *Down came the apples, mmmmm ... they were good!*

Next, peel, core, and slice the washed apples. Pour about an inch of water into a saucepan, and invite children to help drop the apple slices in. Cover the saucepan and cook the apples over a stove or hot plate until soft, about seven to 10 minutes. Allow them to cool thoroughly.

BEGIN

Transfer the cooked apples to a large bowl and help children use wooden spoons to stir them. Talk about the changes: "Those chunky slices are all mushy now. Look how smooth our applesauce is getting." "The apple pieces were white, but the cooked apples are almost brown." Encourage children to sprinkle in a little cinnamon and/or lemon juice. Take time to notice the new smells.

Now the applesauce is ready! Invite a few children to spoon small amounts into paper cups. Other children might enjoy putting a spoon in each cup and setting them on the snack table. Talk about the taste as you sample the sauce. When everyone has finished, help children decorate additional paper cups with stickers. Spoon in the applesauce, and cover the cups with pieces of plastic wrap so children can bring them home.

Remember
- Put out extra foods for tasting during preparation.
- If possible, encourage children to watch the cooking process from a safe distance. Talk about what they see, hear, and smell as the apples cook.

BOOKS
Here are books about the five senses.

- *The Touch Me Book* by Pat and Eve Witte (Golden Press)

- *Nibble, Nibble* by Margaret Wise Brown (Addison-Wesley)

- *The Country Noisy Book* by Margaret Wise Brown (Scott, Foresman & Co.)

COOKING

A twos adventure in the wonderful world of cooking!

GO BANANAS!

Aim: Children will use fine-motor and self-help skills as they develop confidence and self-esteem.

Group Size: Two or three children.

Materials: A whole banana, a large unbreakable bowl, small cutting boards or plates, plastic knives, and napkins. For additional recipes: a blender, small plastic bowls, and plastic spoons.

Ingredients: One banana for every 2 children. For additional recipes: 2 cups milk; 1 teaspoon cinnamon, and 1/4 cup each wheat germ and finely chopped nuts; 2 tablespoons raisins; and 1/4 cup plain yogurt.

In Advance: Slice bananas in half. Slit peels slightly to make peeling easier.

GETTING READY

Gather your group and talk about bananas. Pass around a whole banana, and notice its color, texture, shape, and weight. Pull back the peel and talk about the inside. Discuss different ways children have seen bananas prepared — cut up, in fruit salad, in ice cream, etc. Explain that today, your group will have a chance to make their own banana snacks.

BEGIN

Wash hands thoroughly and gather at the kitchen or snack table. Offer each child a small cutting board or plate, a plastic knife, and a banana half. Encourage children to peel the bananas themselves. Demonstrate how to safely slice or "saw" the fruit using a plastic knife. (Help children to hold the knife by the handle and avoid touching the serrated part.) As children finish slicing, invite them to sample one or two banana pieces and put the rest in a large bowl. Sprinkle the bananas with a very small amount of lemon juice and use in one of the following recipes.

Milk shakes: Combine the banana slices (equivalent of two bananas) with 2 cups milk. Blend them in a blender until smooth. Makes six 4-oz. servings. *Banana Crunchies*: In an unbreakable bowl, mix 1/2 teaspoon cinnamon with 1/4 cup wheat germ and 1/4 cup finely grated nuts. Sprinkle the mixture over the bananas and serve in bowls. *Banana-Raisin Mix*: Combine the banana slices with 2 tablespoons raisins and 1/4 cup plain yogurt. Mix and serve in small bowls.

Involve children in cleanup. Encourage them to throw away trash, bring utensils to the sink, and wipe the table with small sponges.

Remember

- Encourage children to do as much of the preparations as they safely can.
- Emphasize handwashing and cleanup as integral parts of your cooking routine.

BOOKS

Here are books to share with twos.

- *Nibble, Nibble* by Margaret Wise Brown (Addison-Wesley)

- *The Very Hungry Caterpillar* by Eric Carle (World)

- *1,2,3* by Tana Hoban (Greenwillow Books)

COOKING

Enjoy making these muffins as much as eating them!

MAKING MUFFINS

Aim: Children will use fine-motor skills to add and mix ingredients, as well as the senses of taste and smell.
Group Size: Four children.
Materials: Paper muffin liners; custard cups or a muffin tin; a large mixing bowl and three small bowls; a mixing spoon and several smaller spoons; measuring cups and spoons; an oven; a permanent marker; and paper towels.
Ingredients: 1 cup flour, 1/2 teaspoon baking powder, 1/2 teaspoon baking soda, 1/4 teaspoon vanilla, 1/4 cup vegetable oil, 1/4 cup unsweetened frozen apple juice concentrate, 1 ripe banana (mashed), raisins, cinnamon, and peaches canned in their own juice or fresh peaches (peeled and diced).

GETTING READY

Put raisins, cinnamon, and peaches in separate bowls with a spoon in each. Place these bowls, along with all of the other materials and ingredients, in the center of your worktable. Preheat the oven to 400 degrees Fahrenheit.

BEGIN

Invite several interested children to wash their hands so they can join you in making muffins. Using a permanent marker, write each child's name on the bottom of a muffin liner. Place a second liner inside each one and place them in custard cups or a muffin tin. With children's help, measure, pour, and mix all of the dry ingredients in the large mixing bowl. As you do, talk about the ingredients (the colors and textures) and the various measurements (cups and teaspoons). Then add the remaining ingredients, taking time to smell and talk about each one. Ask children if they like what they smell, and be prepared for various answers. Encourage discussion and opinions. Help children use a spoon to fill their muffin liners halfway. Then talk about the ingredients in the bowls. Name, smell, and note the texture of each. Invite children to decide if they would like to sprinkle raisins, peaches, and/or cinnamon onto their batter. (About one spoonful of raisins and/or peaches, and 1/8 teaspoon of cinnamon are just the right amounts.) Help children stir in their choices. Clean up together using damp paper towels while your muffins cook for about 20 minutes.

Remember
▪ Allow muffins to cool before serving. Check names on the

bottom to make sure each child has his or her own muffin.
▪ Twos have definite likes and dislikes. Encourage tasting as children desire.
▪ Be prepared for messes by keeping plenty of paper towels handy.

BOOKS

| Add these books about foods to your library. | ▪ *Eating Out* by Helen Oxenbury (E.P. Dutton) | ▪ *Sam's Cookie* by Barbro Lindgren (William Morrow & Co.) | ▪ *What Do I Taste?* by Harriet Ziefert and Mavis Smith (Bantam Books) |

COOKING

Mmmmmm, try this for delicious fun!

FRUIT DIPPERS

Aim: Children will make choices and use fine-motor skills as they experience different flavors.

Group Size: Up to five children.

Materials: A vegetable peeler and an apple corer/slicer (for adult use), paper plates or bowls, plastic forks and knives, napkins, a serving spoon, and a cotton ball for each extract used (see below).

Ingredients: A variety of fruit (bananas, apples, grapes, pears, and strawberries), a large container of plain vanilla yogurt (enough for each child to have about a half cup), and several flavoring extracts and spices (lemon, almond, and cinnamon).

In Advance: Peel, core, and slice pears and apples. Slice each banana into thirds or fourths, leaving the peel for children to remove. Break bunches of grapes into smaller clusters of three to six grapes. Wash and hull strawberries. Place the fruits on paper plates.

Dab each flavoring extract on a separate cotton ball and place all the cotton balls on one paper plate. Set place settings at the table with paper plates, plastic forks and knives, and napkins. Place the plates of food, the extracts, cotton-ball flavoring samples, and bowls of yogurt in the center of the table. (You might ask children to help you with any or all of these tasks.)

BEGIN

As children observe and help you set up for the activity, invite them to join you at the table for something to eat. Let them sample one, some, or all of the fruits available. Encourage children who choose a banana to slice it into bite-sized pieces using a plastic knife. Offer help when needed. Then place a spoonful of yogurt on a plate. Show children how to pierce a piece of fruit with a fork and dip it into the yogurt, then taste it.

Now show children the flavoring extracts and invite them to smell the different scents on the cotton balls. Using one extract, flavor some yogurt, put a small portion on your plate, and taste. Exclaim, "Yum, this tastes like lemon! I wonder what a banana would taste like dipped in this? Would you like to make your yogurt taste like lemon (or another flavor)?" Encourage children to sample several kinds, and ask them which they like best. Talk about which fruits taste good with which flavors. Allow children to experiment, but not be wasteful. When each child is finished, help him or her wipe face and hands with a napkin and clean up.

Remember

▪ Often, young children have a difficult time accepting new ideas about food. Give them time and don't force anyone to participate. Allow them to eat all they need of the foods they choose.

▪ Try serving water with this snack. It will satisfy the thirsty, and won't detract from the flavors.

▪ A drop or two of the extracts should be enough. Too much can ruin the taste. (You might experiment ahead of time.)

BOOKS

Twos will love these books about tastes.

▪ *Let's Eat* by Gyo Fujikawa (J.B. Communications)

▪ *Cheese, Peas, and Chocolate Pudding* by Betty Van Witsen (Scott, Foresman & Co.)

▪ *What Do I Taste?* by Harriet Ziefert and Mavis Smith (Bantam Books)

COOKING

Sour? Salty? Sweet? Here are different foods to eat!

HAVE A TASTING PARTY!

Aim: Children will experience characteristics of different foods and practice descriptive language.

Group Size: Whole group.

Materials: Ten to 12 paper plates or bowls; markers; napkins; and plastic forks and spoons.

Ingredients: The following foods for tasting: naturally sweet foods such as raisins, grapes, and applesauce; salty foods such as bouillon, saltines, and peanut butter on toast; and sour foods such as dill pickles, grapefruit, and lemon wedges.

In Advance: Select two or three kinds each of sweet, salty, and sour foods. (See the ingredients list for suggestions.) Prepare them as needed, and place on separate paper plates or small bowls. Have enough food for everyone to have a small taste of each kind.

GETTING READY

Gather children for a "tasting party." Explain that you're going to put out many different kinds of foods. Children can choose to taste all the foods, some of them, or even none of them. Let everyone know it's okay to like or not like the tastes.

BEGIN

Put out the plates of sweet foods first. Name them together, then take a small taste of each. Describe the foods as you eat them, modeling several ways to say the same thing: "Look how wrinkled the raisins are! They have little lines in them. Mmmm, mine tastes sweet! Does yours taste sweet?" Also, ask questions that encourage children to think and make connections: "Does this applesauce taste like the kind we made? Do you ever eat applesauce at home?" Allow time for children to think about your questions, though they often won't verbalize their answers. Continue until everyone who is interested has tasted all the sweet foods.

Now repeat the activity using the salty and sour foods. In each food category, emphasize the words "taste," "sweet," "salty," and "sour."

Have a Taste Test for Textures!

Another day, focus on "Foods That Feel Different." Try some sticky foods such as jam on bread, dried fruits, and melted cheese; crunchy foods such as apples, carrots, and crackers; and soft foods such as yogurt and cream cheese. Talk about the different textures.

Remember

▪ The main purpose of this activity is for twos to experience the tastes and textures of foods. Be sure not to make assumptions or be judgmental about the foods children like. They might like everything, or nothing, or only lemon wedges!

▪ Be cautious about asking children to decide if they like a particular food. A child who answers "no" may be unwilling to taste it again in the future.

BOOKS

Share these good food books.

▪ *Food* by Sara Lynn (Aladdin Books)

▪ *The Very Hungry Caterpillar* by Eric Carle (Putnam Publishing Group)

▪ *At the Table*, a Children's Board Books Series book (Price, Stern, Sloan)

COOKING

This cooking idea is perfect for breakfast, lunch, or snack!

HOLD A TOAST BUFFET!

Aim: Children will make choices and practice language and fine-motor skills.

Group Size: Three or four children.

Materials: Spoons; paper plates and/or bowls for food; napkins; aluminum foil; a baking sheet; and plastic knives.

Ingredients: Whole-grain bread and an assortment, or all, of the following ingredients: cottage cheese, cream cheese, all-fruit spread, peanut butter, sliced bananas, grated cheese, cinnamon, and raisins.

In Advance: Cut bread into quarters and place on a baking sheet. Put the remaining ingredients on separate plates or in bowls. Arrange them in groups of three or four on a low "buffet" table, along with napkins for each child (if possible, a different table from where children eat). You might invite children to help with the preparations.

About 10 minutes before the activity begins, pre-heat the oven to 400 degrees Fahrenheit.

GETTING READY

Put out the bread quarters and invite children to talk about them — how they look and feel, ways they can be eaten, etc. Include toast in your discussion, and talk about how bread becomes toast. Then put the bread into the toaster or oven. Invite children to guess how it will look when it is toasted. When it is ready, place each piece on a separate paper plate and add them to the buffet table.

BEGIN

Show children the snack buffet you've set up. Talk about how each ingredient looks, tastes, and smells.

Demonstrate how to choose food from the buffet. Begin by taking a plate with toast, then move to the first group of ingredients. Name them all, choose one, and spread or sprinkle it on your toast. Repeat with the other groups. Encourage children to follow you through the buffet line, making their own food selections. Help, if necessary, as they assemble their snacks.

As children sit and enjoy their food, encourage them to have a conversation. You might talk about the combinations they've created, or other foods that could be on a buffet table. Invite them to make and eat additional toast creations if they choose.

Remember

▪ By arranging food in groups, you help twos make choices without feeling overwhelmed. Three choices, or four at most, usually work well.

BOOKS

Try these resources for good cooking ideas.

▪ *Learning Through Cooking* by Nancy Ferreira (R&E Publications)

▪ *Come and Get It: A Natural Foods Cookbook for Children* by Kathleen Baxter (Children First)

▪ *Cooking With Kids* by Caroline Ackerman (Gryphon House)

COOKING

Enjoy the sensory experiences this gelatin cooking project provides.

JIGGLING GELATIN

Aim: Children will follow directions, use fine-motor skills, and explore with their senses.

Group Size: Three or four children.

Materials: An eight-inch square pan and a spatula; plastic knives and spoons; and paper plates.

Ingredients: Three packages of unflavored gelatin, two cups orange juice, and several bananas. (Serves eight children.)

In Advance: To prepare the gelatin, bring one and one-half cups orange juice to a boil. While the juice is heating up, soften three packages of unflavored gelatin in the remaining one-half cup orange juice. When the juice comes to a boil, combine it with the gelatin mixture and stir until the gelatin is dissolved. Pour the mixture into the pan and chill until firm. Cut the bananas into thirds (one third per child), and cut a small slit in the peel of each third to make peeling easier.

Optional: You can also make different flavors and colors of gelatin using grape, apple, or cranberry juice.

BEGIN

Help children wash their hands. Then gather at the kitchen or snack table. Invite children to watch as you cut the firmed gelatin into eight large squares. Using a spatula, put the squares on paper plates and serve one to each child. As you cut and serve, talk with the children about the gelatin. Help them notice its color and shape. Ask if anyone has eaten gelatin before. Was it the same color or a different color?

Give each child a plastic knife and demonstrate how to use it to cut the gelatin. As children are cutting their own pieces, encourage them to touch the gelatin with their fingers. Talk about how it looks and feels. Then offer each child a banana section. Encourage everyone to peel his or her banana, slice it using a plastic knife, and place a banana slice on each piece of gelatin they've cut up.

Eat the gelatin and banana snack with plastic spoons. As you eat, notice the way the gelatin moves on the spoon. Talk about the taste.

Later in the day, do a movement activity based on gelatin. Encourage children to remember how the gelatin moved on the plate and on the spoon. Then move your arms, legs, and whole bodies like the gelatin.

Remember

▪ This recipe provides a healthy alternative to prepared gelatin mixes, which usually contain a lot of sugar.

BOOKS

These books offer other suggestions for cooking with children.

▪ *Fancy, Sweet, and Sugar Free* by Karen Barkie (St. Martin's Press)

▪ *Peter Rabbit's Natural Foods* by Arnold Drobin (Frederick Warne)

▪ *Once Upon a Recipe* by Karen Greene (New Hope Publishing)

COOKING

Choose ingredients to make your own pizzas!

PERSONAL PIZZAS

Aim: Children will make choices and use fine-motor skills to create their own snack.

Group Size: Three or four children.

Materials: Magazine pictures of pizza; plastic spoons; small plastic knives (optional); aluminum foil; a baking sheet; several unbreakable bowls; paper plates; napkins; and an oven.

Ingredients: English muffins (one half per child); grated cheese (two kinds, if possible, such as mozzarella and Parmesan or Romano); tomato sauce; and three kinds of vegetables such as peppers, tomatoes, and mushrooms.

In Advance: Cut the vegetables into small pieces. Place each in a separate bowl or plate. Pour the tomato sauce into two small bowls and separate the English muffins into halves. About 10 minutes before you begin the activity, preheat the oven to 400 degrees Fahrenheit. Put aside small portions of the vegetables, cheese, and sauce for children to taste as they cook.

GETTING READY

Talk about the uncooked ingredients and invite children to take sample tastes. Explain that these are the ingredients to make pizza, and today children are going to make their own!

If possible, use magazine pictures to illustrate your conversation. Later, some children might even want to make a "pizza collage."

BEGIN

Offer each child half an English muffin on a small plate. Help them spread a thin layer of tomato sauce on the muffins using a plastic spoon, and sprinkle on the grated cheese. Then invite them to choose which vegetables they want to put on their pizzas. Encourage and help them talk about their actions as they follow each step.

When the pizzas are ready to bake, help children place them on a baking sheet covered with aluminum foil. Tape children's names next to their pizzas. Place the baking sheet in the oven and bake eight to 10 minutes or until the cheese melts. Let them cool, then serve as a nutritious lunch or snack. As you eat, talk about how the ingredients tasted before you cooked them and how they taste now.

Remember

▪ Some twos have had little experience in making choices. Be patient as they decide. Offer suggestions, but avoid making decisions for them.

BOOKS

These books offer additional cooking suggestions.

▪ *Gingerbread Tales* by David Gamon (AD Bradgon)

▪ *Cup Cooking: Individual Child Portion Picture Recipes* by Barbara Johnson and Betty Plemons (Gryphon House)

▪ *Super Snacks* by Jean Warren (Warren Publishing House)

 ### COOKING

Celebrate warm-weather foods with this tasting party.

MOUTHFULS OF MELON!

Aim: Children will practice observation and descriptive-language skills as they explore the appearance of different melons.
Group Size: Three or four children.
Materials: Watermelon, honeydew, and cantaloupe (or other seasonal melon); a sharp knife; spoons or scoops; a large bowl; paper plates and plastic spoons; chart paper; and markers.

GETTING READY

Gather your group together and, if possible, read *The Very Hungry Caterpillar* by Eric Carle. Then talk about foods children like to eat. Do they have special favorites when the weather is warm? Invite children who have been on outdoor picnics to share their experiences. What kinds of food did they eat?

BEGIN

Put the melons out on a table. Begin a discussion by asking children to share their observations. Help them compare the colors, textures, shapes, and sizes. How are they the same? How are they different? Next, open the melons and continue making comparisons. What is the same and different about the insides? Are they the same color inside as outside? What about the seeds? Encourage children to use words to describe what they see. Record everyone's observations on chart paper.

Together, wash your hands and the tabletop. Help children use spoons or melon scoops to scoop out the inside. Offer tastes of each kind and ask children to share their reactions. How do the melons taste? Which do they like best? Again, record their observations.

Finish scooping out the melons and put the pieces into a large bowl for snack. (For fun, try cutting the watermelon into the shape of a basket and using it for serving all of the melon pieces.)

When you eat snack, take out the chart paper and refer to it as you continue your melon discussion.

Remember
▪ Ripe melons taste better and are easier to scoop. To check, gently press near the top. Melons should be slightly soft and have a somewhat sweet smell.
▪ You may want to repeat this activity using blueberries, strawberries, raspberries, and blackberries.

BOOKS

Add these books to your summer foods discussion.

▪ *Blueberry Pie* by Louise and Richard Floethe (Charles Scribner's Sons)

▪ *Waiting for Cherries* by Ann Himler (Harper & Row)

▪ *Once We Went on a Picnic* by Aileen Fisher (Thomas Y. Crowell)

COOKING

Help children fix something delicious!

LET'S MAKE PEANUT BUTTER

Aim: Children will use sensory, comparative, and observation skills as they see the changes that occur when peanuts are ground to make peanut butter.

Group Size: Three or four children.

Materials: A small paper bag; paper for recipe cards; a blender, bowls, spoons, and a spatula; paper plates, napkins, and tongue depressors or ice cream sticks; measuring spoons and cups; and shelled peanuts, crackers, and/or celery sticks.

Ingredients: Roasted peanuts in their shell (enough to make one cup of shelled peanuts); vegetable oil (about 1 1/2 tablespoons), and salt.

In Advance: Prepare recipe cards to show the following steps: 1) Measure 1 1/2 tablespoons vegetable oil and 1 cup shelled peanuts. 2) Pour into a blender. Blend. 3) Sprinkle with salt. 4) Blend again.

Illustrate the steps with pictures from magazines. If possible, laminate the cards for durability.

GETTING READY

Play a guessing game. Bring a small paper bag of unshelled peanuts to group time. Ask, "What do you think could be in this bag?" Shake it and talk about the sound it makes. What things make that sound? Pass the bag around but ask children not to look inside. When everyone has finished guessing, reach in the bag and pass one peanut to each child. Talk about what they have and whether children have seen peanuts with their shells on before. Take out a few shelled peanuts for comparison. Invite children to crack the shell and eat the peanut inside.

BEGIN

At the cooking table, give everyone a small pile of peanuts. Help them crack the shells and remove the brown skins from the nuts. Provide a bowl to hold the nuts.

As you work, talk about textures. Compare the shells with the peanuts. What words describe them — *bumpy? smooth?* Which part do we eat? How many nuts did children find in each shell? Compare the sizes.

Read your recipe cards together. Now follow the steps to make peanut butter. Watch as the blender changes the peanuts from crunchy to smooth.

When the peanut butter is ready, invite children to help serve it. Arrange cut celery sticks and crackers on a plate. Put out a small amount of peanut butter. Offer tongue depressors or ice cream sticks to use for spreading. You can also make two batches of peanut butter, one crunchy and the other smooth. Take time to talk about how the two peanut butters look. Do they smell different? Taste different? Do they feel different in children's mouths? Take a vote on which type children like better.

Remember

▪ Ask children to sit down, and place the blender so they can see it easily from their chairs. Keep it unplugged as you pour in ingredients. When you are ready to blend, insist that children remain seated. Ask them to touch their chairs as a reminder to keep their hands a safe distance away.

BOOKS

Share these fun books about food.

▪ *Eat!* by Diane Paterson (Dial Books)

▪ *Rain Makes Applesauce* by Julian Scheer (Holiday House)

▪ *Each Peach Pear Plum* by Janet and Allen Ahlberg (Scholastic)

COOKING

Fresh bread and jam taste even better when you make them yourself!

SNACKING ON BREAD AND JAM

Aim: Children will exercise fine-motor skills and experiment with textures as they cook.

Group Size: Two or three children.

Materials: For jam: mashers, plastic knives, paper plates, a mixing bowl, measuring cups, a large spoon, and a saucepan. For bread: a loaf pan, enough vegetable shortening to grease the pan, and a cake tester. You'll also need napkins or paper plates and small plastic spoons or knives.

Ingredients: For jam: 6 bananas and 1/4 cup lemon juice. For bread: Frozen bread dough.

GETTING READY

Ask whether children have eaten bread with jam before. What does it taste like? What are some different ways they have tried it? On toast? With peanut butter? What jam or jelly flavors do they like best? If possible, read *Bread and Jam for Frances* by Russell and Lillian Hoban (Scholastic) or one of the books recommended below.

BEGIN

Banana Jam: Help children peel bananas and slice half of each one onto a paper plate. Show them how to use a masher and have fun mashing away. Scoop the mashed banana into a bowl. Then repeat the process with the rest of the banana halves and add them to the bowl.

Next, help children measure 1/4 cup of lemon juice, add it to the bowl of bananas, and mix well.

Allow the banana mixture to sit for about one hour. Then simmer it for 30 minutes on medium heat, stirring often. As the jam cools, prepare the bread!

Baked bread: To save time, try baking a quality brand of frozen bread dough. (Children can still observe the rising process as the dough defrosts.)

Follow the directions on the label for defrosting, greasing the loaf pan, letting the dough rise, and baking. Encourage children to predict how high they think the bread will rise.

Now set the table with napkins or paper plates and plastic knives or spoons. Enjoy the bread together while it is still fresh and warm from the oven. Help children spread jam on their slices of bread. Serve warmed apple juice, too, for a special cozy treat!

As you eat, talk about textures. How does the bread feel? How does the jam feel? Encourage children to use descriptive

words such as *sticky*, *soft*, *warm*, and *crumbly*.

Invite children to join in Frances' favorite *Bread and Jam for Frances* chant:

> *Jam on bread*
> *Jam on toast*
> *Jam is what I like most!*

Remember

- Be sure children wash their hands before preparing food!
- Extend this into a two-day project by preparing bread from scratch. You could try several kinds of jam, and invite family members or another group to your bread and jam party.

BOOKS

Here are books about bread.

	■ *I Did It* by Harlow Rockwell (Macmillan)	■ *The Bake-Off* by Lorinda Cauley (Putnam Publishing Group)	■ *The Giant Sandwich* by Seth Agnew (Doubleday)

COOKING

Cook them, stuff them, eat them — potatoes are great fun!

ONE POTATO, TWO POTATO

Aim: Children will use fine-motor skills and learn about vegetables as they prepare a nutritious snack.

Group Size: Four or five children.

Materials: Old magazines, scissors, glue, a large piece of oaktag, a box of toothpicks, five shallow bowls and a large mixing bowl, water, spoons, plastic knives, forks or potato mashers, and vegetable scrubbers.

Ingredients: Baking potatoes (one for every two children); a little milk (for mixing); several kinds of raw vegetables; and juice or milk.

In Advance: Send a note home explaining to families that you will be talking about and eating vegetables. Ask families to send in one baked potato and one portion of a vegetable that tastes good raw, such as carrots, green peppers, or cauliflower. Or you could do the preparations yourself.

GETTING READY

During snack or lunchtime, begin a discussion about nutritious foods. Talk about how vegetables are one kind of food that helps our bodies grow and stay healthy. Encourage children to tell you about vegetables they have eaten. Later, you might help children cut out pictures of vegetables from old magazines and glue them to a large piece of oaktag paper.

BEGIN

Gather in your kitchen or dramatic-play area. Put out baked potato halves and raw vegetables and invite children to make a snack. Help them use vegetable scrubbers to wash the raw vegetables, and plastic knives to dice them. Put the raw vegetables aside and offer each child a baked potato half. Help them scoop out the insides, leaving the skin intact. Spoon the potato "meat" into the bowl and take turns mashing it up. (You might want to add just a little milk to make the mashing easier.) Mix in the diced vegetables. Help children spoon some of the potato and vegetable mixture back into the potato skins so they have a mound of mixture in each half. Pass out napkins and juice or milk and enjoy a nutritious meal!

Remember

▪ Some three-year-olds can learn to use knives to cut vegetables safely. Take time to teach them how to hold knives by the handles and keep the flat sides of vegetables on the table. You might want to boil vegetables slightly to make them easier to cut.

▪ To reinforce your nutrition activities, prepare and serve nutritious foods in your setting. Keep sweets to a minimum and encourage parents to do the same.

BOOKS

Enjoy recipes from these good cookbooks.

▪ *Easy Cooking for Kids* by Sandra Sanders (Scholastic)

▪ *Kids Are Natural Cooks* by Parents' Nursery School (Houghton Mifflin)

▪ *Vicki Lansky's Kids Cooking* by Vicki Lansky (Scholastic)

COOKING

Cooking can be "egg-citing"!

DEVILED EGG NESTS

Aim: Children will use fine-motor and creative-thinking skills as they create and cook.

Group Size: Four or five children.

Materials: Experience-chart paper, a marker, small spoons, a mixing bowl and spoon, a grater, plastic forks and knives, small paper bowls, and pictures of birds and nests. (If you want to boil the eggs with children you'll need a large pot, a hot plate, and a timer.)

Ingredients: One hard-boiled egg per child; 5 or 6 tablespoons mayonnaise or low-fat yogurt; 2 or 3 teaspoons prepared mustard; small amounts of paprika and pepper; a small head of lettuce; grated carrots; 2 cups celery, cut in thin strips; and one raw egg (optional).

In Advance: Prepare a recipe chart for deviled eggs:

1. Fill a pot with water and boil eggs for 20 minutes. Then cool the eggs.
2. Peel the eggs.
3. Cut in half the long way and scoop out yolks.
4. Place yolks in a mixing bowl.
5. Blend with mayonnaise or low-fat yogurt (about five to six tablespoons or until mixture is smooth).
6. Add mustard (one teaspoon per 10-12 eggs).
7. Mash ingredients together using a small fork.
8. Add pepper or paprika to taste.

Read the chart through together and invite children to help illustrate it.

GETTING READY

Begin a discussion by talking about where eggs come from. Also talk about birds and their nests. Explain that a nest is a bird's "house," where eggs can grow. If possible, show pictures of birds' nests. Bring the discussion back to eggs and ask children, "What are some different ways you can fix eggs?"

BEGIN

Gather your group around a table in your kitchen or snack area. Carefully pass around a whole raw egg and a hard-boiled egg. Talk about them and compare. How are they the same? How are they different? Encourage children to use descriptive language. Now open both eggs and continue making comparisons.

Next, boil the eggs and cool them, or offer each child a hard-boiled egg. Help children peel the eggs, slice them in half the long way, and scoop out the yolks into a big bowl. Then follow the steps to mix the egg yolks.

When the mixture is finished, demonstrate how to carefully place a small amount back into each egg white. Offer children small paper bowls and grated carrots, celery strips, and lettuce leaves to create "nests" for their eggs. (Leave out pictures of nests for children who might want to look at their shape and construction again.) When the nests are finished, put in the eggs. Eat them now or chill them in the refrigerator until snacktime.

Remember

- Eggs are high in both protein and cholesterol. While cholesterol can present a health risk for adults, it is not a problem for most children.
- Peeling hard-boiled eggs is a challenge for many threes. Remember, it's more important for children to exercise their fine-motor skills than make tidy nests.

BOOKS

Add these books to your discussion about eggs.	▪ *The Egg* by Dick Brauna (Methuen)	▪ *Scrambled Eggs Super!* by Dr. Seuss (Random House)	▪ *The Eggs* by Aliki (Pantheon Books)

COOKING

Make snack a cheese extravaganza!

CHEESE FEAST, ANYONE?

Aim: Children will compare and sample different cheeses.
Group Size: Whole group.
Materials: Paper plates, blunt plastic knives, napkins, crackers, and the cheeses listed below.

GETTING READY

Talk about cheese at group time. Ask children to think of ways they have seen cheese served — on grilled cheese sandwiches, pizza, salads, by itself, etc.

Introduce some of these cheeses to your group: cheddar, mozzarella, cream cheese, cottage cheese, Parmesan, Swiss, Muenster, and feta. Invite children to identify the cheeses they know. Which ones have they eaten before? How were they fixed? Encourage children to look at and compare how the cheeses are alike and how they're different.

BEGIN

Set out paper plates, plastic knives, spoons, and cheese. Ask children, "Which cheeses can we cut with a knife?

Which can we scoop with a spoon?" Encourage children to cut and scoop, then arrange the cheeses on crackers for snack.

Before you eat, take a few minutes to talk about how the colors and textures look.

Invite children to sample one piece at a time. Talk about how different cheeses taste and feel in your mouth. Ask children if they have a favorite. Enjoy snack as you continue to taste and talk. Now clean up snack the same way you prepared it — together!

Later, or another time, assemble small amounts of different cheeses again and invite children to smell them. Talk about and compare smells. You may even want to bring a cheese known for its strong odor, such as blue or Gorgonzola.

Remember
▪ Involve families in the activity by inviting children to bring a favorite cheese from home.
▪ Some children may be reluctant to try new foods. Encourage them to taste the cheeses, but don't insist.

BOOKS

Here are three good stories about food.

▪ *Joey's Cat* by J. Burch (Viking)

▪ *Is This My Dinner?* by Irma Black (Albert Whitman)

▪ *Dig, Drill, Dump, Fill* by Russell Hoban (Greenwillow Books)

COOKING

You are invited to a formal tea. Menu: Herbal sun tea, rainbow sandwiches, and mint salad.

TEA FOR TWO

Aim: Children will use fine-motor and imaginative-play skills as they cooperate to prepare a special snack.
Group Size: The whole group.
Materials: Unbreakable teapots, cups, saucers, small plates, serving trays, and vases; and a small tablecloth or flat sheet to use as a tablecloth. Cooking materials: a one-gallon jar with a top, and plastic butter knives. Dramatic-play props: "fancy" dress-up clothes such as white gloves, suit jackets, ascots, bow ties, boas, and costume jewelry.
Ingredients: Herbal tea bags (any flavor); sugar-free spreadable fruit (three different flavors and colors); thin, sliced whole wheat bread; a peeled cucumber; 1 pint yogurt; and 1/2 cup chopped mint.
In Advance: Place the props mentioned above in your dramatic-play area. Keep the ingredients and cooking materials ready.

GETTING READY

Talk about tea parties. Explain that some people have a special afternoon snack called "tea time." Sometimes tea time is a very fancy event where people wear dressy clothes and eat special foods. Talk with children about any times they got very dressed up, perhaps for a wedding. You might ask how they felt and acted at these events. If children have no experience with such occasions, help them imagine what it would be like. Ask what they think they would wear and what they might eat. Then one day, when children are involved in playing "tea party," suggest that you make a real tea time together.

BEGIN

Gather children in three groups — one group to make tea, another to make sandwiches, and a third to make salad. (This can be done at the same time if you have enough staff members, or at three different times.) *To make herbal tea*: Fill a one-gallon glass jar with water. Place three or four tea bags in the water. Put on the lid and leave out in bright sunlight for a few hours. *To make rainbow sandwiches*: Help children spread cream cheese and a layer of all-fruit spread on a piece of wheat bread. Place a second piece of bread on top and add a second layer of cream cheese and a second layer of fruit spread — this time, a different color. Add a third piece of bread, a third layer of cream cheese, and a third color fruit

spread, then a fourth piece of bread. Help children use butter knives to cut the bread into triangles. To make mint salad: Invite children to chop up cucumbers and put the pieces into a bowl with the chopped mint and yogurt. Mix together, and refrigerate until ready to serve.

Take time for everyone to select a few dress-up props to wear. Then enjoy your special tea-time foods together!

Make It an Occasion!

Make invitations for family members or other groups of children. Invite everyone to come in their dress-up clothes. Some children may want to serve the food on trays. Others can create centerpieces or draw picture menus. If the weather is right, take your special tea time outside!

BOOKS

Here are three perfect books for tea time.

- *Busy Week* by Eugenie Fernandes (Ladybird Books)

- *Grandmother's Chair* by Ann Herbert Scott (Clarion Books)

- *Rosy's Garden* by Satomi Ichikawa (Philomel Books)

ACTIVITY PLAN
READY-TO-USE TEACHING IDEAS FOR THREES

 COOKING | **Threes will feel a sense of accomplishment as they make sundaes all by themselves!**

YUMMY YOGURT SUNDAES

Aim: Children will reinforce their self-help, creative-thinking, and problem-solving skills as they create their own snack.

Group Size: Three or four children.

Materials: One large paper cup or bowl and one plastic spoon per child; paper plates and serving spoons for sundae ingredients; and napkins.

Ingredients: A large container of plain, low-fat yogurt and any combination of the following: raisins, chopped nuts, chopped fresh fruit (bananas, apples, berries, etc.), sunflower seeds, unsweetened shredded coconut, pieces of rice cake, granola, and wheat germ.

In Advance: Ask a few interested children to help you wash and chop the fruit and prepare other ingredients as needed. Place each ingredient on its own paper plate. Line them up on a low table so children can reach them easily, and place a serving spoon on each. Put out the yogurt with its serving spoon, and plastic spoons.

GETTING READY

Gather your group and talk about sundaes. How are they different from plain ice cream? What are some special things people put on sundaes? Explain that today, you are all going to make yogurt sundaes!

BEGIN

Wash hands, then look at and discuss all the sundae ingredients. Encourage children to use expressive-language skills as they name and describe each one. Invite children to take a small taste of any ingredient that they've never tried before. Explain, as you demonstrate, how to make sundaes. "First I'm serving myself a big spoonful of yogurt. Then, I'll put whichever ingredients I want on top of the yogurt. I'm picking bananas, granola, and coconut." Remind children to use the serving spoon that is with each ingredient and return it to its spot.

While everyone is eating their very own sundaes, have fun talking about the different combinations.

Remember

▪ Some children may go overboard adding ingredients. Try controlling portions by using small "taster" spoons like those found in ice cream parlors.

▪ Vary your presentation depending on your group's cooking experience. For beginners, emphasize that this is a snack they can make all by themselves. You might also encourage children to practice stirring by mixing their sundaes. For veteran chefs, stress that today they can make up their own "secret" recipes. Some might even like to dictate their recipes to you.

BOOKS

| Here are more great stories about food. | ▪ *Stone Soup* by Ann McGovern (Scholastic) | ▪ *Pancakes, Pancakes* by Eric Carle (Alfred A. Knopf) | ▪ *I Did It!* by Harlow Rockwell (Macmillan) |

COOKING

Learn about shapes and eat them, too!

LET'S MAKE SNACK SHAPES

Aim: Children will work with, sort, and match shapes, as well as exercise fine-motor skills.

Group Size: Two or three children.

Materials: A few pieces of stiff paper or cardboard; adult scissors; four large paper plates; plastic knives; napkins; and basic-shape cookie cutters.

Ingredients: Crackers in the shapes of squares, triangles, and circles (enough for your whole group for snack); margarine, cream cheese, and/or all-fruit jam; and about half a loaf of whole-grain bread (optional).

In Advance: Cut out large circles, squares, and triangles from stiff paper or cardboard. Make at least two or three of each shape to use for sorting and matching activities. Also cut out a small circle, square, and triangle to use as labels.

GETTING READY

Place your cut-out shapes in a pile, and gather your group for a few shape activities. Encourage children to look at and feel the sides, corners, and curves of the different shapes. Help them describe what they see and feel. Try a game in which children point to a shape from the pile and find something else in the room to match it. Invite them to sort the shapes into separate piles.

BEGIN

Arrange four large paper plates on your snack table. On one, place a variety of circle-, square-, and triangle-shaped crackers. Label the other three plates using the small shapes that you cut out. Then invite interested children to wash their hands and help you sort the crackers for snack. Point out the plates and labels, and show everyone how to match the crackers to the appropriate plates.

When children have finished sorting, demonstrate how to use a plastic knife to spread a small amount of cream cheese, margarine, or all-fruit jam onto the crackers. (Remind the children to put the crackers back on the matching plate.) Suggest that they leave a few crackers plain for added variety. At snacktime, invite children to choose the cracker shapes they want. They may select all one kind, or one of each!

Another day, or as a variation, show children how to use the cookie cutters to "press" the whole-grain bread into shapes. Lightly toast the bread shapes. (This will make spreading easier.) Talk about how the bread changed as it was heated. Then encourage everyone to match the shapes into pairs. Spread on a topping or two and make your own shape sandwiches!

Remember

- Use shape names frequently, but keep in mind that it's more important for threes to recognize and match shapes than to name them.
- Make sure children are safely away from heat sources.

BOOKS

These books are useful in discussing shapes.

- *Shapes* by Jan Pienkowski (Simon & Schuster)

- *The Parade of Shapes* by Sylvia Root Tester (Child's World)

- *Anno's Journey* by Mitsumasa Anno (Putnam Publishing Group)

COOKING

Eat the "fruits of your labors" with this special group activity.

FRIENDSHIP FRUIT SALAD

Aim: Children will develop self-esteem, fine-motor skills, and a sense of community as they contribute to this "no-cooking" project.

Group Size: Your whole group.

Materials: Pictures of different kinds of fruit; a large serving bowl and spoon; small bowls and plastic spoons for everyone; and plastic knives.

Ingredients: One piece of fresh fruit from each child (apples, bananas, pears, mangoes, grapes, etc.); additional fresh fruit; and about 1/3 cup lemon juice.

In Advance: Send a note home to families two or three days before you plan to do this activity. Explain that your group will be making a Friendship Fruit Salad, and families can help by contributing one fresh fruit that their child likes to eat. Be sure to include the date. You might also invite family members to join you in making and eating the salad.

As the fruit arrives, label each piece with the child's name and store it appropriately.

GETTING READY

Gather everyone in your group together. Ask children to think about a time when they shared something with a friend. Talk about how it felt to share, and also how their friends might have felt. Explain that you are going to make a special snack — one that everyone will share. Each person will help by bringing a piece of fruit from home. Then,

together, you'll mix all the fruit into a salad.

BEGIN

Give each child the fruit he or she brought in and gather together. Invite children, one at a time, to show and talk about their fruit. (Don't forget to show yours, too!)

Then work in small groups to prepare the salad. Wash hands well, and help children wash their fruit. Demonstrate how to cut safely with a plastic knife, using a sawing motion. Sprinkle lemon juice on apples, pears, or bananas to retard browning. When the fruit is cut, help children transfer it to the serving bowl. Offer children large spoons to help mix the fruit together. When the last group has added their fruit, your salad is ready!

At snacktime, encourage children to serve themselves from the Friendship Fruit Salad bowl. Talk about the salad as you eat it. "Mmmmm, I'm eating some of Mario's apple now! It tastes great with Kim's grapes!"

Remember

▪ Be sure to have extra fruit on hand in case someone forgets his, and also to add variety to your salad.

▪ Cooking projects can be great opportunities for family members to help out. Make sure you offer any family assistants a few guidelines about conducting group activities with young children.

BOOKS

Here are good books about good friends to check out of your library.

▪ *Come Play With Us* by Anne S. O'Brien (Henry Holt & Co.)

▪ *I Want That!* by Anne S. O'Brien (Henry Holt & Co.)

▪ *George and Martha* by James Marshall (Houghton Mifflin)

 COOKING

Nutritious, quick, and easy — scones are fun for fours.

WHOLE WHEAT SCONES

Aim: Children will use math skills to measure, divide, and compare; science skills to investigate ingredients and predict changes; and fine-motor skills to pour, mix, knead, roll, and cut.

Group Size: Four or five children.

Materials: Experience-chart paper and a black marker; a baking pan; an oven; measuring cups and spoons; a large mixing bowl; mixing spoons; a sifter; rolling pins; cookie cutters that are 2 1/2 inches in diameter; and a timer.

Ingredients: Seven ounces whole wheat flour; 1/2 teaspoon salt; 3 teaspoons baking powder; 2 ounces margarine at room temperature; 1/2 cup milk; vegetable shortening to grease pan; additional margarine to serve with baked muffins; and milk or juice for everyone.

GETTING READY

Make a recipe chart together. Read aloud as you write down and number the following recipe steps:

1. Wash hands and tabletop.
2. Preheat oven to 425 degrees Fahrenheit.
3. Measure all ingredients.
4. Sift flour, salt, and baking powder into bowl.
5. Add margarine and mix.
6. Add milk and mix again.
7. Dust tabletop with flour.
8. Roll dough until it's 1/2 inch thick.
9. Spread shortening on baking sheet.
10. Use cookie cutters to cut dough into circles.
11. Put circles on baking sheet.
12. Set the timer for 15 minutes.
13. Place scones in the oven.

Invite children to draw or cut out pictures to illustrate the steps on your chart.

BEGIN

Hang the recipe chart at children's eye level. Together, gather ingredients and utensils and put everything out on a table. Take time to examine each ingredient. Invite children to pour some whole wheat flour into a clear plastic container. Pass the container around so everyone has a chance to look, smell, and touch a bit of flour.

Follow the recipe, helping children "read" and perform each step through step 12. Before adding each ingredient, ask everyone to predict how it might change the look, smell, feel, or taste of the dough. Encourage children to test their predictions.

When the dough is arranged on the baking sheet, make sure an adult puts it into the oven. Bake at 425 degrees for 15 minutes. Serve warm with margarine for spreading and cups of milk or juice.

Remember
- Children like to taste foods as they cook. Have extra ingredients on hand in separate containers just for that purpose. When taste-testing, limit children to small bites.
- Practice kitchen safety. Many four-year-olds are ready to watch, from a safe distance, as you set the oven temperature, place the baking pan in the oven, set a timer, and remove the cooked scones. However, always stress the need for safety and adult supervision in a kitchen.

BOOKS

Here are books and films about bread.	▪ *The Story of Bread* (film by SVE Educational Films)	▪ *Bread, The Staff of Life* by Walter Buehr (William Morrow & Co.)	▪ *Bread and Jam for Frances* by Russell Hoban (Harper & Row)

COOKING

Enjoy this cooperative "cooking" activity!

SPIN A SALAD

Aim: Children will work cooperatively as they develop fine-motor skills and experiment with meal planning.

Group Size: Three or four children at a time.

Materials: A large piece of oaktag paper; a piece of cardboard; paint and a paintbrush; one pair of adult scissors and several pairs of children's scissors; old magazines; brass brads (double-pronged paper fasteners); and food for snack from the specific food group, fruits and vegetables.

In Advance: Cut a very large circle from the oaktag paper, and an arrow shape from the cardboard. (The arrow should be about 1/4 of the diameter of the circle.) Invite children to paint the arrow. Once it dries, show them how to push a brad through the center of the arrow and the center of the circle. Fasten it so the arrow can spin.

GETTING READY

During a meal or snacktime, join children in a discussion about what they are eating. You might choose a time when you are having fruit for snack. As children name their foods, respond with an answer that gives them information about food groups: "Yes, you have a banana. A banana is a fruit. Does anyone else have some fruit? What are some other fruits you like?"

BEGIN

Put out old magazines and scissors and encourage children to cut out all the pictures of fruit they can find, or draw pictures of fruit. Together, sort the fruit pictures into piles — all the apples together, all the grapes, etc. Bring out the oaktag circle and glue or paste the like fruits together, each having its own section. Invite children to spin the arrow and name the fruit.

Make a fruit salad. Invite each child to spin the arrow. Explain that the fruit the arrow lands on will be one ingredient in the salad. Make a list of your ingredients together, and the next day fix this salad together for snack.

Spin a Meal!

Use this activity to talk more about food groups and nutrition. Focus on each of the other food groups — dairy products, meats and dried beans, bread and grains — one at a time. Then glue or paste pictures of each group in four different places on the oaktag circle. Again, invite children to spin the arrow and list the foods it lands on. Use your list to plan a well-balanced lunch!

Remember

▪ Healthy eating habits last a lifetime. Share nutrition information and healthy recipes with children's families, and invite family members to share theirs.

▪ Be sure to use magazines that show many different kinds of foods, including foods that are eaten by people from various cultural backgrounds.

BOOKS

| These books about foods are wonderful for four-year-olds. | ▪ *My Eating Book* by Jane Gelbard and Betsy Bober Polivy (Grosset & Dunlap) | ▪ *Patrick Eats His Dinner* by Geoffrey Hayes (Alfred A. Knopf) | ▪ *What's on My Plate?* by Ruth Belov Gross (Macmillan) |

COOKING

Pound and shape dough to make these soft, chewy pretzels!

DESIGNING PRETZELS

Aim: Children will use fine-motor, descriptive-language, and creative-thinking skills as they design pretzel shapes.

Group Size: Four or five children.

Materials: Clean trays, measuring cups and spoons, 3 mixing bowls, a mixing spoon, an egg beater, a baking sheet, a small pastry brush, and pictures of pretzels (optional).

Ingredients: 1 1/2 cups warm water, 1 envelope yeast, 4 cups flour, 1 tablespoon honey (to activate the yeast), 1 teaspoon salt, and 1 egg. (Or substitute 2 loaves of thawed frozen dough, 1 teaspoon salt, and 1 egg.)

In Advance: Preheat the oven to 425 degrees Fahrenheit.

GETTING READY

If possible, read *Pretzel* by H.E. Rey, or show children pictures of pretzels. Talk about pretzels and their shapes. Help children describe different shapes they have seen. Talk about the kinds of pretzel shapes children might like to make and eat.

BEGIN

Ask children to wash their hands and help make pretzel dough. Mix the warm water, yeast, and honey, and set aside for five minutes. Mix the salt and flour in a separate bowl. Add the yeast mixture to the salt-and-flour mixture and stir them together. (If you are using frozen bread dough, you won't need to mix.) Then beat the egg and set it aside.

Give everyone a clean tray to work on. Help each child take a handful of dough to shape into his or her own unique design. Explain to children that they can experiment with various shapes and designs before they decide which ones they want to bake into pretzels. The more they handle their dough now, the fatter their pretzels will be.

When the shapes are completed, ask children to brush them with the beaten egg to make them shiny. Bake for 12 minutes and serve fresh from the oven. As you eat, use descriptive language to talk about the shapes, tastes, and textures.

Remember
- Prepare dough in small groups of two or three.
- Plan to eat pretzels very soon after removing them from the oven because pretzels become hard as they cool.
- You might want to put mustard on your pretzels, or try a dip made of plain yogurt and onion soup mix.

BOOKS
Share these other books about fun foods.

- *Green Eggs and Ham* by Dr. Seuss (Random House)
- *Pancakes for Breakfast* by Tomie DePaola (Harcourt Brace Jovanovich)
- *In the Night Kitchen* by Maurice Sendak (Harper & Row)

COOKING

Go "nutty" over these cooking experiences!

NUTS!

Aim: Children will practice problem solving as they observe, describe, and cook with nuts.

Group Size: Four to six children.

Materials: Large index cards and a marker; a measuring cup and spoons; a nutcracker; a blender; several bowls; a spatula; and paper plates and napkins for everyone.

Ingredients: One cup each of the following kinds of nuts, plus a few extra for tasting: Brazil nuts, almonds, walnuts, cashews, peanuts, hazelnuts, and macadamia nuts; corn oil (1 1/2 tablespoons per cup nuts); salt; crackers; a small amount of peanut butter; and celery (optional).

In Advance: Prepare a picture recipe card for each of the following steps: 1) place 1 cup shelled nuts in a blender; 2) add 1 1/2 tablespoons corn oil; 3) blend until smooth; 4) add 1/4 teaspoon salt; 5) blend again. (You might ask children to help you illustrate the cards.)

GETTING READY

Gather children to talk about nuts — their various colors, textures, and shapes. How are they alike? How are they different? Crack open a few of the kinds still in the shell and invite children to taste them. Talk about how the insides look and feel.

BEGIN

Show your group a few whole peanuts and a small amount of peanut butter. Ask children how they think they could make the peanuts "turn into" peanut butter. Leave plenty of time for thinking. Respond positively to all comments. Then explain that today you'll try one way to make peanut butter, using a blender.

Wash hands, then shell the peanuts together. Follow the steps on your recipe cards. When the peanut butter is ready, unplug the blender, remove the peanut butter using a spatula, and transfer it to a bowl. Offer everyone a small taste.

Now talk about the other nuts and ask children if they think these could be made into butters. To test your prediction, follow the recipe cards using other types of nuts. Make as many nut butters as you choose, being sure to label each kind.

At snacktime, put out the nut butters in small bowls. Try them with crackers and/or celery sticks and compare the tastes and textures.

Remember

▪ Help children use nutcrackers to open the shells of harder nuts.

▪ For safety's sake, be sure children watch the blender from a distance.

▪ Children might like to "vote" for their favorite nut butter — a great opportunity for graphing!

BOOKS

Try these books for additional fun cooking ideas.

▪ *Creative Food Experiences for Children* by Mary Goodwin (Center for Science in the Public Interest)

▪ *Cup Cooking* by Barbara Johnson and Betty Plemons (Early Educators Press)

▪ *Kids Are Natural Cooks* by Parent's Nursery School (Houghton Mifflin)

COOKING

Sing your way through this simple recipe!

A MUSICAL COOKING ASSEMBLY LINE

Aim: Children will practice fine-motor skills as they cooperate to create a nutritious snack.

Group Size: Four or five children.

Materials: A large, unbreakable serving plate; napkins and small paper plates for everyone; a few plastic knives; several small bowls and spoons; and a box of toothpicks.

Ingredients: Bananas (one half per child); an 8-oz. container of yogurt; and about 1/2 cup of any or all of the following: wheat germ, unsweetened shredded coconut, granola, and graham cracker crumbs.

In Advance: Place the wheat germ, coconut, granola, and graham cracker crumbs in separate bowls. Arrange them in a line on a low table. Place a plate and the toothpicks at one end of the table, and the serving plate at the other.

GETTING READY

Before you start, make sure everyone has clean hands. Then begin a discussion about the foods on the table. Invite children to name any they recognize, and tell about where they have seen and tasted them. Compare the foods' colors, shapes, and sizes.

BEGIN

Prepare your assembly line. Encourage children to help peel the bananas and slice them into thick circles. Place the slices on a plate next to the toothpicks. Next, put the yogurt into a bowl and set it next to the bananas.

Explain that today everyone will help make snack in a special way. Help children form a line, and demonstrate the assembly process. Stick a toothpick into a banana slice, then continue down the line, dipping the slice into the yogurt, then any of the other ingredients. At the end, place the finished product on the unbreakable serving plate. Go back to the beginning of the assembly line to repeat the procedure. Encourage children to follow your lead and choose the ingredients they want to use.

Sing this song as you move through the line!

The Banana Treat Song
(Tune: *The Wheels on the Bus*)
Dip the banana in the yogurt,
In the yogurt, in the yogurt,
Dip the banana in the yogurt,
Then roll it in the wheat germ.

Continue the song, describing each of the choices. When all the bananas slices have been dipped, give each child a paper plate. Invite them to take a few banana slices to eat for snack.

Remember
▪ Later, try putting other repetitive actions to music, such as dressing to go outside, cleaning up, etc. Singing can enhance your routines, and offers children great practice in verbalizing their actions.

BOOKS
| These books combine cooking and music. | ▪ *Take a Bite of Music, It's Yummy!* by Mary Ann Hall (NAEYC) | ▪ *Cricket's Cookery* by Pauline Watson (Random House) | ▪ *Recipes and Rhymes* by Elaine Bastable (Heinemann Educational Books) |

COOKING

Read, make, eat, and be the Very Hungry Caterpillar!

THE HUNGRY CATERPILLAR FRUIT SALAD

Aim: Children use fine-motor and creative skills to prepare a nutritious fruit salad.

Group Size: Four to six children.

Materials: *The Very Hungry Caterpillar* by Eric Carle (Collins and World), one paper plate and one plastic knife per child, paper towels, experience-chart paper, and markers or crayons.

Ingredients: For two servings: one small banana; two small, cored, unpeeled apples cut into at least six pieces each, or one large apple cut into 12 pieces; two lettuce leaves; and four raisins.

GETTING READY

Share the book *The Very Hungry Caterpillar*. Talk about everything the caterpillar in the story eats. If children have some experience with caterpillars, discuss whether they think real caterpillars eat these things. Ask, "How do you think the caterpillar felt after it ate all those foods? How would you feel if you ate all that food?" Pass the book around and encourage children to flip through the pages. Explain that you will be doing an activity during which everyone can make caterpillars and butterflies out of food.

BEGIN

With children, write and illustrate a recipe chart to follow as you prepare the fruit salad. On a large piece of experience-chart paper, list each ingredient — 1/2 banana; six apple slices; one lettuce leaf; and two raisins. Next to each, invite a child to draw or paste pictures showing what is needed to make one salad. Then list and picture materials — a plastic butter knife, a paper plate, a napkin or paper towel to work on, etc. Last, write and illustrate step-by-step directions on how to prepare Caterpillar Fruit Salad:

1. Wash hands and tabletop.
2. Peel banana.
3. Use knife to cut banana in half the long way.
4. Save 1/2 banana for a second salad or another snack.
5. Peel off and wash one lettuce leaf.
6. Place lettuce on your paper plate.
7. Lay your banana half on top of lettuce.
8. Add apple slices as legs and raisins as eyes to create a caterpillar.

9. See if you can arrange lettuce, banana, apples, and raisins into a butterfly!
10. Eat!

Help children read and follow the recipe chart. Collect ingredients and materials together, and then encourage children to do the preparation.

Remember

▪ Avoid showing children a picture of the finished salad in either caterpillar or butterfly form. Let them use the ingredients to form their own unique interpretations.

▪ If possible, include children in your trip to buy materials and ingredients.

▪ Try to have extra ingredients available for children who want to make more than one salad.

Caterpillar Fruit Salad
½ banana
6 apple slices
1 lettuce leaf
2 raisins
a plastic butter knife
a paper plate
a napkin

BOOKS

Add these children's books about butterflies and caterpillars to your shelves.

▪ *How to Hide a Butterfly and Other Insects* by Ruth Heller (Grosset & Dunlap)

▪ *I Like Butterflies* by Gladys Conklin (Holiday House)

▪ *I Like Caterpillars* by Gladys Conklin (Holiday House)

COOKING

Everyone can feel special when you make "group soup."

FRIENDSHIP SOUP

Aim: Children will have an opportunity to develop self-esteem as they contribute to a group cooking project.

Group Size: Whole group.

Materials: Pictures of vegetables, several plastic serrated knives and vegetable peelers, a soup pot, a long wooden spoon, a ladle, cups, plastic spoons for everyone, masking tape, and a marker.

Ingredients: One vegetable from each child in your group, plus a few extra; canned or powdered soup stock (to make about 1/2 cup per person); bread or crackers; and pepper (optional).

In Advance: Send a short note to families asking them to contribute a fresh vegetable that their child likes. (Get these in a few days early so you can fill in with other vegetables to balance your soup.) Be sure to include the date you'll need them. As the vegetables arrive, use tape to label them with children's names.

GETTING READY

Talk about your Friendship Soup. Explain that everyone will help make it by bringing in and preparing the vegetables. Discuss the different kinds of vegetables children might bring. If possible, use pictures to illustrate your discussion.

BEGIN

On the day of the activity, invite each child to show the vegetable he or she brought. Talk about the different colors, shapes, and sizes.

Fill your soup pot with enough stock to make about 1/2 cup of liquid per person. Then work in small groups to prepare the soup. Ask children to wash their hands, then give each his own vegetable to prepare. Help children wash, peel, and cut the vegetables into pieces. Add the pieces to the pot. Be sure to demonstrate the safe way to use plastic knives and peelers.

When all the vegetables are in the stock, place the pot on a hot plate or stove. Bring the liquid to a boil, then simmer for one hour or until the vegetables are soft. As the soup cooks, notice the changes in texture, color, and aroma. Supervise carefully as you help children use a wooden spoon to stir the soup. You might want to taste it and add a little pepper. Then serve it for snack with crackers or bread.

Remember

▪ Encourage everyone to talk about the vegetables they bring in. Be sure to find out the names of vegetables you are unfamiliar with, and how to prepare them.

▪ Consider boiling root vegetables — potatoes, carrots, etc. — ahead of time to make cutting easier.

BOOKS

Read these books about friends and sharing.

▪ *The Great Flower Pie* by Andrea Di Nota (Bradbury Press)

▪ *Best Friends* by Myra Berry Brown (Golden Gate)

▪ *George and Martha* by James Marshall (Houghton Mifflin)

COOKING

Your mission: finding ways to scramble eggs!

HOW MANY WAYS CAN YOU SCRAMBLE AN EGG?

Aim: Children will practice creative-thinking, problem-solving, and expressive language skills.

Group Size: Four to six children.

Materials: Experience-chart paper and a marker; a heat source such as a hot plate, electric frying pan, or stove; a frying pan; a medium-sized mixing bowl, paper plates, and plastic forks for each child; a wooden spoon; and an assortment of the following tools: forks, spoons, a hand-held egg beater, an electric mixer, a wire whisk, baby-food jars, and chopsticks.

Ingredients: One egg for each child, butter or margarine for cooking, and catsup (optional).

GETTING READY

Discuss the different ways children like to eat eggs. Mention scrambled eggs, and ask if children have ever seen them being prepared. Brainstorm real and pretend ways to scramble eggs, and record children's responses on experience-chart paper.

BEGIN

Introduce the various mixing tools you have collected and invite your group to name and discuss them. Encourage children to think of their own names for tools that are unfamiliar and describe how they might be used. Predict which tools you think will beat eggs best. Record predictions on another piece of experience-chart paper.

Now give each child an egg and a medium-sized bowl. Help children crack their eggs into the bowls, then invite them to try any or all of the tools to use for beating. (The baby-food jar is for shaking the eggs.) Talk about the changes in the eggs as you beat them.

Ask children to observe which tools work best and which beat the egg the fastest. Record their comments, then compare this list with your predictions. Talk about how close the predictions are to the results.

Review safety precautions, then begin cooking. Add about half a tablespoon of butter or margarine to the cooking pan and melt it over low heat. Add one child's egg to the pan. Keep the heat low and supervise closely as each child carefully uses a spoon to stir his or her own egg.

Eat your scrambled eggs for snack. Offer catsup to those who would like to try it.

Remember

▪ This activity works best if children begin with simple utensils, such as forks or chopsticks, then move on to the more complex tools. Be sure an adult holds the electric mixer.

▪ Talk about how children's predictions compare with actual results, rather than whether they are "right."

BOOKS
Enjoy these "egg" books together.

▪ *The Eggs* by Aliki (Pantheon)

▪ *Green Eggs and Ham* by Dr. Seuss (Random House)

▪ *Scrambled Eggs Super!* by Dr. Seuss (Random House)

COOKING

**Fat bread, flat bread, bread with a hole —
people eat all kinds of bread!**

HAVE A BREAD-TASTING PARTY

Aim: Children will build language skills and multicultural awareness as they taste and compare breads.

Group Size: Whole group.

Materials: A large mixing bowl and spoon; a frying pan with lid; a spatula; napkins and paper plates (at least two for each child); an oven, electric frying pan, or hot plate; and a variety of breads such as pita, corn tortillas, pumpernickel, whole wheat, Irish soda bread, pan bread, challah, croissants, steamed buns, etc.

Ingredients: Vegetable oil spray, 1 cup sweet butter, 1 cup buttermilk, 1 teaspoon salt, 1 tablespoon shortening, corn meal, melted butter to fry bread, extra butter or margarine, all-fruit spread, and/or additional bread toppings.

In Advance: Choose an assortment of breads that reflect the cultural backgrounds of your group or your community. (Remember, everyone has a culture!) You might talk with parents or others to learn more about their cultures.

GETTING READY

Together, read *Bread, Bread, Bread* by Ann Morris. Talk about the many different kinds of breads, and all the different people who eat bread.

BEGIN

Gather at your kitchen or snack table. Show children the breads you've brought in, and ask if anyone has eaten these breads at home. Encourage children to talk about the breads they are familiar with — how the breads taste, what other foods they eat with the bread, etc. Take time to examine and describe each kind. Compare and talk about color, shape, and texture.

Give each child a paper plate and pass around small tastes of each bread. Talk about the tastes as you eat. Use descriptive language such as *sweet*, *doughy*, *chewy*, *dry*, and *soft*. Offer children additional pieces of their favorites. Serve with butter or other appropriate toppings.

Make Homemade Pan Bread

Make this Native American bread recipe with children:

Mix sweet butter, buttermilk, salt, shortening, and corn meal together in a large bowl. Use enough corn meal to achieve a thick, doughy consistency. Coat the frying pan with vegetable oil spray and set on a heat source at medium heat. Melt a small amount of butter. Pour the dough into the pan. Cover the pan, and cook until the pan bread is brown on one side. Turn it with a spatula and brown the other side. Let the bread cool. Serve on paper plates with butter or all-fruit spread.

Remember

▪ Avoid overgeneralizing when you talk about cultures. For example, rather than saying, "Arab families eat pita bread," you could say, "Ellie eats pita bread at home. Her family is Arab." Point out that not all Arab families — in this country or others — eat pita bread, and many non-Arab families do.

▪ Involve families! Invite family members to send in the kinds of bread they like to eat, or bread they make at home. Perhaps a child's family member would like to visit your program, bake bread, and talk with the children about his or her culture.

BOOKS

Add these books about similarities and differences to your library.

▪ *Bread, Bread, Bread* by Ann Morris (Scholastic)

▪ *This Is the Way We Go to School — A Book About Children Around the World* by Edith Baer (Scholastic)

▪ *We Are All Alike ... We Are All Different* by the Cheltenham Elementary School Kindergartners (Scholastic)

COOKING

Explore the many foods made from apples!

SAUCE, BUTTER, CIDER, JUICE

Aim: Children will use language and thinking skills to compare different apple products.

Group Size: Four or five children.

Materials: Large sheets of construction paper to make a graph; paper to make circles for "voting"; a marker; three different kinds of apples — red, yellow, and green; a variety of apple products, such as applesauce, apple juice, apple butter, apple yogurt, dried apples, cinnamon apples, apple cider, and apple cider vinegar, as well as a picture of each one; bread cut into bite-sized pieces; and plastic knives, paper plates, cups, plastic spoons, and napkins for everyone.

In Advance: Prepare a taste-test graph to record children's likes and dislikes. Divide large sheets of construction paper into two- or three-inch-wide columns. Make one column for each apple product, with a label or picture at the top that represents the food. Cut small (one-inch) circles with smiling or frowning faces for children to vote. Be sure you have enough room on the chart for every child to vote for each product.

GETTING READY

Gather your group and show them the three apples. Talk about how they are alike and how they are different. Together, think of as many apple products as you can and discuss the ones children most like to eat.

BEGIN

Invite a few children to help you arrange an "Apple Buffet." Look at all the apple products. Encourage comparative and descriptive language as you notice the differences. Are apple pieces visible? How have the apples changed? Next, help children match each product to the pictures on the graph. Explain that the graph will be your record of which products children like and don't like.

Offer children a small amount of each food to taste, beginning with a piece of fresh apple. (Spread the apple butter on the bread pieces.) Discuss the tastes. Encourage children to use descriptive words such as *sweet* or *sour*, rather than just saying "bad" or "good." As children taste, show them how to "vote" by placing a smiling-face circle in the columns of the foods they like and a frowning face in the columns of foods they don't like.

Later, look at the graph together. Talk about how to "read" the faces on the graph. Which foods do children like most? Which do they like least?

Remember

▪ Avoid apple products with lots of added sugar.

▪ Fours need many experiences with the concept of graphing. Try voting for other favorites.

BOOKS

Here are good books to enhance your discussion about apples.

▪ *A Tree Is Nice* by Janice Udry (Harper & Row)

▪ *Apple Orchard* by Irmengarde Eberle (Henry Z. Walck)

▪ *Buttons and the Magic Apples* by Josephine Newbury (John Knox Press)

COOKING

Try this no-cook activity with your five-year-olds. It's a group effort!

FRUIT SHAKES

Aim: Children will use language and social interaction skills, as well as the math skills of comparing and counting.
Group Size: Four or five children.
Materials: A blender, a few plastic knives, a measuring cup, mixing spoons and paper cups for each child, experience-chart paper, and markers.
Ingredients: For 6-8 children: one cup fresh or canned unsweetened fruit; 2 cups plain low-fat yogurt, 1 6-oz. can unsweetened frozen apple juice concentrate, and your favorite fruit for everyone to taste.
In Advance: Write notes to send home, asking families to send their child's favorite fruit.

GETTING READY

Gather a small group together, and ask children to name some of their favorite things to eat. Share a few of your favorite foods, too. Talk about favorite fruits, and offer each child a taste of yours. Explain that you're going to be making a snack with fruit. Then send home the notes asking parents to send in their child's favorite.

BEGIN

Ask children if they'd like to show the fruits they brought from home. Give them time to talk about the shapes, colors, and smells. Ask questions that don't call for just one response: "Which fruits do you think smell good? Which colors of fruit do you like the best? What do you think we'll need to do before we eat them? How can we clean the fruits you brought?"

Now it's time to make fruit shakes. Choose one type of fruit at a time. Help children use plastic serrated knives to cut the fruit into chunks. (You may have to chop it into still smaller pieces.) Then, together, place the chopped fruit, yogurt, and juice concentrate in the blender, and whip the mixture on high speed until smooth. Groups can make different flavors and sample them at snack. Encourage children to discuss the different tastes and talk about their favorite flavors.

Build a Theme Around Favorites

Talking about favorite fruits and flavors can be just the beginning. You might also encourage children to make "favorite" books that include drawings and pictures cut from magazines, or have a conversation about favorite toys and encourage them to bring a favorite from home to share.

Remember

▪ Most children feel special when they have opportunities to talk about their favorite things. Asking children to bring something from home is a great way to enhance these positive feelings.
▪ Five-year-olds like to be able to do things themselves. Allow children to do all the preparation with as little adult supervision as possible.
▪ Fives also enjoy making comparisons, and they learn much about mathematical thinking in the process.

BOOKS

Enjoy these fun food-related books at storytime.

▪ *The Biggest Sandwich Ever* by Rita Golden Gelman (Scholastic)

▪ *Each Peach Pear Plum* by Janet and Allan Ahlberg (Scholastic)

▪ *Strawberry* by Jennifer Coldrey and George Bernard (Silver Burdett)

COOKING

Try this simple way to make a delicious fruit snack!

BROILED FRUIT CRISP

Aim: Children will use fine-motor, expressive- and receptive-language, measurement, and observation skills.
Group Size: Three or four children.
Materials: Plastic serrated knives and paper plates for each child, measuring cups and spoons, a mixing bowl, an oven-proof baking dish, a broiler, and a blender.
Ingredients: Crisp: 2 cups fresh fruit, such as apples or peaches; 2 tablespoons lemon juice; 6 tablespoons rolled oats; 4 tablespoons flour; 1/2 teaspoon cinnamon; and vegetable oil to mix. Fruit whipped cream: A few pieces of fresh or unsweetened canned fruit, and 1 cup heavy cream.

GETTING READY

Discuss the ingredients together. Encourage children to describe how each looks and feels. Then explain that when you cook something, the ingredients often change. Ask, "What do you think happens when you put a piece of bread in the toaster? How does it change? What do you think happens to water when you put it in the freezer? How does it change?" Ask children to share examples of changes they have noticed. Talk about how the heat of a stove or the cold of a freezer changes food. Explain that today you are all going to make something called a crisp. Together you can watch the way each of the ingredients changes.

BEGIN

First help children cut the fruit into pieces. Together, measure the lemon juice and mix it with the fruit in an oven-proof dish. Measure and mix the rolled oats, flour, and cinnamon. Add just enough oil to make a crumbly dough. Ask, "What do you think would happen if we added too much oil? What could we mix in to help?" "What could we use more of if we wanted to make our crisp taste spicier?"

Take the mixture and sprinkle it over the fruit. Ask children, "How do you think the crisp will look when it comes out of the broiler? How might it be different from when we put it in? How will the fruit look?" Broil for three to four minutes about six inches away from the heat. Carefully remove from heat and observe the changes. Ask, "What happened? Why do you think the ingredients changed?"

The crisp tastes best slightly cooled and served with a little homemade whipped cream. Here is a simple recipe for making fruit whipped cream and another opportunity to observe change:

Take a few pieces of fresh or unsweetened canned fruit and whip in a blender until smooth. Take time to observe the changes the fruit goes through from fresh to whipped. Then ask children to examine 1 cup of heavy cream. Ask, "How do you think we could make this into whipped cream?" "How will it look then?"

Whip 1 cup of heavy cream at high speed until peaks form. Then add 1/4 cup of the blended fruit. This is a good chance for children to observe change because it happens slowly and they can see different stages as the liquid thickens.

Remember

When cooking with five-year-olds:
- Make sure they wash their hands before working.
- Allow them to do many of the steps of the process themselves, but closely supervise stove cooking and the use of the blender.
- Take time to do this project slowly so children can make in-depth observations and predictions.
- Help children observe change in all parts of their lives. Encourage them to point out changes in the weather, the room, themselves, etc.

BOOKS

Looking for more healthy recipes? Here are some sources.

- *Fancy, Sweet, and Sugar Free* by Karen Barkie (St. Martin's Press)

- *Peter Rabbit's Natural Foods Cookbook* by Arnold Drobin (Frederick Warne)

- *Super Snacks* by Jean Warren (Warren House Publishing)

COOKING

This recipe lets fives see food changes in action!

HEALTHY FRUIT AND NUT GORP

Aim: Children will use observation, fine-motor, and group-interaction skills as they observe changes in food.

Group Size: Three or four children.

Materials: Several paper plates, several large blocks, cheese cloth, a few paper or cloth towels, an apple corer/slicer, a few paper clips, buttonhole thread or kite string, a cooking tray, a spatula to remove seeds and nuts from the tray, and a medium-sized mixing bowl and spoon.

Ingredients: One bunch seedless grapes (green grapes work best); about 5 Macintosh or any other variety of soft apple; about 1/4 cup lemon juice; 3/4 cup each raw sunflower seeds and raw nuts such as almonds or cashews (avoid peanuts); and 1 tablespoon vegetable oil.

GETTING READY

Gather children together and introduce the raw ingredients. Invite children to talk about them. What are some ways they have seen these foods fixed? How have they eaten them? Where do these foods come from? Offer children a taste of each raw item. (Set samples of raw ingredients aside, so children can use them later to compare.)

BEGIN

Explain that for this recipe, you will be cooking or drying the raw ingredients. Then in a few days, when the ingredients are ready, you'll mix them together to make a healthy snack!

Making Raisins. Begin by asking children, "Where do raisins come from?" (Many will be surprised to learn that a raisin is a dried grape!) Invite children to wash the grapes and remove them from their stems. Gently but thoroughly dry the grapes and place them on paper plates. Cover with cheese-cloth. Place the plates on blocks so air can circulate around them, and put them in a sunny spot. Watch and wait for about four days. The raisins will be leathery and pliable when done.

Making Dried Apples. Ask children to wash and dry the apples. Place the apple corer/slicer on the apple and press down slowly to make slices. Ask interested children to help. (To retard browning, dip slices in lemon juice.) Make "needles" out of paper clips and attach the thread or kite string to the closed end. Then demonstrate how to gently push the tip of the paper clip through the center of the white part of an apple slice. Hang these to dry near a sunny window. The

apples should be dried in about four or five days.

Roasting Nuts and Seeds. Help children oil the bottom of a cooking tray or pan. Sprinkle on the nuts and/or seeds and toss lightly. You or another adult can then place the tray in the oven. Bake at 300 degrees Fahrenheit for about 20 minutes, or until lightly browned.

When all the ingredients are ready, gather together again to observe them. Compare the dried or cooked ingredients to raw ones. How are they the same? How are they different? Invite children to mix the ingredients together in a bowl. Now you can eat the healthy snack you made from raw food!

Remember

▪ Demonstrate appropriate ways to handle cooking utensils so children learn to respect their safe usage. Carefully supervise use of the apple corer/slicer.

BOOKS

Here are some cookbooks to add to your collection.

▪ *Cook and Learn* by Beverly Veitch and Thelma Harms (Addison-Wesley)

▪ *Once Upon a Recipe* by Karen Greene (New Hope Publishing)

▪ *Cup Cooking* by Barbara Johnson and Betty Plemons (Early Education Press)

COOKING

Here's a way to make a salad and learn more about graphing, too!

CREATE A GROUP SALAD BAR

Aim: Children will use the mathematical skills of counting, comparing, grouping, and graphing as they graph salad ingredients.

Group Size: Both whole group and small group.

Materials: Paper plates and plastic forks for each child, plastic bowls for serving, several plastic serrated knives, experience-chart paper, markers, and pictures of salad ingredients.

Ingredients: Salad ingredients children bring from home, plus a few extra. Optional: oil and vinegar to make salad dressing, and butter and bread for croutons.

In Advance: Use a large sheet of chart or graph paper to make a salad-bar graph. At the bottom of the page, draw or cut out magazine pictures to represent the different ingredients. Above each picture, make a column of boxes that can be colored in. Be sure the boxes are the same size so the graph readily shows "how many."

GETTING READY

Engage your group in a discussion about salad bars. Ask, "Have you ever been to a salad bar? What kind of food is at a salad bar? If we were to make a salad bar here, what foods do you think we should serve in it?" Together, create an experience chart listing the foods suggested.

Send a note to families asking that they contribute an ingredient to your group salad bar. You may want to include a copy of the children's ingredients list for suggestions.

BEGIN

When children arrive with their vegetables, invite them to look for the column representing their ingredient and color in one square for each item they brought.

Help each child wash and prepare (peel, cut, grate, etc.) his or her own ingredient. Together, place the prepared ingredients on paper plates and arrange them on a low table. If desired, a small group of children can make salad dressing while others toast and butter bread for croutons. Encourage children to line up, serve themselves the ingredients they choose, and make their own personal salads. Now dig in!

Discuss the completed graph while children are eating. Emphasize the comparative math concepts of "most," "least," and "same" by asking, "Which ingredients do we have the most of? Least of? Are any the same amount?" Ask children to count the number of different ingredients on their plates. Who has the biggest assortment? Together, think of other questions that can be answered with your graph.

Remember

- Be sure to send notes home early enough so that families have time to shop, then remind them the day before.
- Keep a few extra vegetables on hand for children who don't bring in an ingredient from home.
- Five-year-olds need many experiences with the concepts of "most" and "least." Graphing a hands-on activity is an important method to make these concepts come alive.

BOOKS

Try these cookbooks for more cooking and graphing ideas.

- *Kids Cooking Without a Stove* by Aileen Paul (Doubleday)

- *Easy Cooking: Simple Recipes for Beginning Cooks* by Ann Beebe (William Morrow & Co.)

- *Crickets' Cookery* by Pauline Watson (Random House)

COOKING

All you'll need is a blender to make this simple all-natural treat.

WHAT CAN YOU DO WITH A BANANA? MAKE ICE CREAM!

Aim: Children will use observation, comparison, and fine-motor skills to make this special snack.

Group Size: Four or five children.

Materials: Freezer or picnic chest that will keep ice frozen; a blender, several plastic bowls, and a mixing spoon; experience-chart paper; a marker; and for each child, paper cups, paper plates, plastic serrated knives, and spoons.

Ingredients: Ripe bananas (approximately 1 per child); a little milk; and unsweetened grated coconut, wheat germ, dried fruits, and chopped peanuts for dipping.

GETTING READY

This is a two-day project. On the first day, taste the

bananas and talk about how good they are for keeping bodies healthy. Then brainstorm all the kinds of foods you can make with bananas. Record your list on experience-chart paper under the heading "Banana Foods."

BEGIN

If possible, prepare one of your "Banana Foods" for snack. One simple way is to serve plain bananas with a variety of dipping ingredients, such as unsweetened coconut, wheat germ, chopped dried fruit, and chopped peanuts. Ask for volunteers to help fill bowls with the various garnishes and slice the unpeeled bananas in half crosswise. Then offer each child one banana half. (Save the other halves for later.) Invite children to peel their banana halves and spoon the garnishes of their choice onto their own paper plates. Encourage them to dip and roll their bananas in the goodies as they eat. Talk about the different tastes and textures. See if the group has a favorite.

Together, prepare for tomorrow's banana ice cream by helping children peel the remaining banana halves (1/2 per child). Place the halves in a freezer overnight. Explain that tomorrow you will use the frozen bananas to make ice cream. Talk about how the bananas might look after they are frozen. How will they feel? You might want to write down children's predictions so you can refer to them tomorrow to compare.

Make Banana Ice Cream

Help children take the frozen bananas out of the freezer. Compare them to unfrozen ones and refer back to yesterday's predictions. Are there any changes you didn't predict?

To make the ice cream, help children use plastic knives to "saw" the bananas into chunks. Place them in a blender and blend, adding just a little milk. (Be careful to blend only until the consistency is thick or you will get a milk shake instead.) Serve and enjoy immediately!

Remember

▪ Help children feel important by acting on their ideas. Consider fixing and eating other foods they brainstormed for your "Banana Foods" chart.

BOOKS

Share these books about food and eating.

▪ *The Man Who Didn't Wash His Dishes* by Phyllis Krasilovsky (Doubleday)

▪ *To Market, To Market* by Emma L. Brock (Alfred A. Knopf)

▪ *The Very Hungry Caterpillar* by Eric Carle (Collins and World)

COOKING

Use your sense of taste as you create your own snack food.

MAKE YOUR OWN SNACK MIX

Aim: Children will compare tastes and use creative problem-solving skills as they make their own snacks.

Group Size: Three or four children.

Materials: Paper plates for serving; cups and napkins for each child; tape, small pieces of paper for circles, a large sheet of paper for graphing, markers, a few pencils, and strips of paper; and a picture or sample of each ingredient below.

Ingredients: Small pretzels, raisins, unsweetened cereal, small crackers (oyster or goldfish type), popcorn, seedless grapes, and small cubes of hard cheese to combine for snack.

In Advance: Prepare a taste-test graph. List children's names down the left-hand side of the large paper. Across the bottom of the paper, tape a drawing or sample of each ingredient. Mark off a column for graphing above each ingredient. Cut paper circles and draw smile faces on them. These will be used to "vote" for the tastes the children like best.

GETTING READY

Talk about the sense of taste. Explain that there are four basic tastes: sweet, sour, salty, and bitter. Invite children to tell about the tastes they like best. Make a list of favorite tastes. Then talk about things children don't like to taste. Together, think of food combinations you would not like to try. Suggest a few combinations, like peanut butter and onion sandwiches or lemon yogurt and brussels sprouts!

BEGIN

Help children put each of the foods on separate paper plates. Invite them to take a piece from the first plate and talk about how it tastes. Ask, "How would you describe the way this food tastes? Is it sweet? Sour? Salty? Smooth? Crunchy?" Encourage children to use as many descriptive words as possible. After they've had an opportunity to taste each of the ingredients, ask them to choose two favorites. Give them two smile faces each to cast their "votes" on the graph.

Next, offer each child a large paper cup to create a snack mix by combining their favorite two tastes with other tastes. As you eat, talk about the ingredients children included in their "recipes." Encourage them to compare their creations with others. Some children may even want

to "write" their recipes by drawing their ingredients on strips of paper. These recipes make great send-homes to share with family members.

Remember
- Have fun with the food combinations children would not like to taste. Consider exclaiming "Yuck!" loudly as a group — this allows children to voice their feelings without getting carried away.
- Save time and paper by creating a reusable graph. Use a large piece of plastic, such as an old shower curtain, instead of paper, and mark off columns and boxes using masking tape.

BOOKS

Here are a few books that explore the world of taste.

- *Miss Pennypuffer's Taste Collection* by Louise B. Scott (McGraw-Hill)
- *Everybody Has a House and Everybody Eats* by Mary McBurney Green (Addison-Wesley)
- *Blueberries for Sal* by Robert McCloskey (Viking Penguin)

COOKING

How can you mash a potato? Invite your five-year-olds to find out!

MASHED POTATO PUZZLE

Aim: Children will use problem-solving, fine-motor, expressive- and receptive-language, and social-interaction skills.

Group Size: Three or four children.

Materials: Experience-chart paper; a variety of utensils such as spoons, forks, hand potato mashers, and/or hand potato ricers; a few vegetable brushes; plastic serrated knives; a large pot (for cooking potatoes); and paper plates, plastic forks or spoons, and napkins for each child. (Optional: a small saucepan, a baking pan, a cookie sheet, cookie cutters, and a pastry brush.)

Ingredients: Two red or new potatoes per child, and water for boiling. (Optional: small amounts of butter or margarine, milk, and nuts, seeds, and raisins for decorating.)

GETTING READY

Start a discussion about potatoes by showing children a raw one. (Some children may not recognize a potato if it isn't cooked or frozen.) Pass it around for children to feel. Together, brainstorm a list of ways to prepare potatoes. Write your list on experience-chart paper.

BEGIN

Gather your group of cooks around the table. Ask, "How do you think we can turn these hard things into soft, fluffy mashed potatoes?" Give everyone time to think and make suggestions. Show children the utensils, and ask if they think these could be used for mashing. Invite them to choose a few and try to mash the raw potato. They'll quickly see that this is not going to work. Together, think of ways to make the potatoes softer and ready to mash. Help children discover that the potatoes have to be cooked.

Now it's time to try your cooking solution. After children have washed their hands, ask them to help wash and scrub the potatoes using the vegetable brushes. Then help children carefully cut (or saw) the potatoes into smaller pieces using the plastic serrated knives. Put the potatoes in a pot of water and boil until soft. After they're cooked, drain them and let them cool.

Now pass out the utensils and mash away! Encourage children to figure out which utensils do the best job. (You might want to warm some milk and butter in a saucepan to make the potatoes thinner.) As you work, talk about other times your group solved problems together. Then eat your mashed potatoes!

Try Something New!

If you have leftover potatoes, try flattening them in a low, flat pan and placing them in the refrigerator overnight. They'll harden enough so that the next day children can help you cut them into interesting shapes using cookie cutters. Preheat an oven to 350 degrees Fahrenheit. Place the cutouts on a greased cookie sheet. Dab a pat of butter or a little oil on top of each shape or use a pastry brush to "paint" with melted butter. Add seeds, nuts, or raisins for features and decorations and bake until browned (approximately 15 minutes).

Remember

■ New or red potatoes work best because they do not have to be peeled — their skins are thin and will mash down easily. Plus, using the skin increases the nutritional value.

■ Be sure to include a variety of utensils — some that mash very well, such as potato mashers or ricers, and others that are not well-suited to the task.

BOOKS

Read these books about potatoes.

■ *Potato* by Barry Watt (Silver Burdett)

■ *Potatoes, Potatoes* by Anita Lobel (Harper & Row)

■ *Stone Soup* by Anne McGover (Scholastic)

COOKING

Make a healthy and hearty soup with this fun recipe!

YUMMY CARROT VEGETABLE SOUP

Aim: Children will cooperate and use comparison, fine-motor, and classification skills.

Group Size: Four to six children.

Materials: A large soup pot, mixing spoons and ladles, serrated plastic knives, a hand-held chopper, a few vegetable peelers, a sharp knife (for teacher use), hot pads, and a large bag to put the vegetables in.

Ingredients: 6 carrots, 6 celery stalks, 1 onion, 2 tomatoes, 4 potatoes, 20 green beans, 20 green pea pods, and 6-8 cups water or bouillon.

GETTING READY

Place the bag filled with whole vegetables in the middle of a circle of children. Invite volunteers, one at a time, to take out one vegetable from the bag. Ask children to name each one. Can anyone suggest what to do with the vegetables? Encourage children to name as many foods made out of vegetables as they can. Explain that today you are going to make soup.

BEGIN

Wash hands and talk about safety procedures before you begin cooking. Demonstrate the safe way to use a plastic knife (using a sawing motion), and how to hold the peelers and chopper. Then offer children the vegetables to prepare.

First, wash the vegetables — this is the most enjoyable part for some children! Encourage them to wash each piece very carefully. Then help prepare the vegetables for children to cut. Cut potatoes into slices for easier peeling. Cut the tomatoes into halves and slice carrots lengthwise. Chop the onion so it's ready to add to the soup. Now begin heating the water or bouillon, and turn the vegetable preparation over to the children. Encourage children to do as much preparation as they can.

Add the cut vegetables to the preheated water or bouillon. Simmer for about 30-40 minutes. This recipe serves 20-25 children.

Now it's time to eat! When you serve the soup, be sure it's not too hot. Encourage children to be "vegetable detectives." How many vegetables can they find and name in their soup?

Remember

• Cooking soup is a great way for children — and families — to work together. Consider sending this recipe home and asking families to share their favorite soup recipes. Make a soup cookbook!

• Many children may be unfamiliar with vegetables in their fresh forms. Bring in a few frozen or canned vegetables, such as peas, to compare with fresh.

BOOKS

Read these books while the soup is simmering.

• *Stone Soup* by Marcia Brown (Charles Scribner's Sons)

• *Watch Out for the Chicken Feet in Your Soup* by Tomie DePaola (Prentice-Hall)

• *Nail Soup* by Harve Zemach (Follett Publishing)

COOKING

Any day is great for an applesauce sundae you create yourself!

RECIPE BY ME!

Aim: Children will practice planning, making choices, and using fine-motor skills while creating a healthy snack.

Group Size: Three or four children.

Materials: A large pot, a few vegetable peelers and plastic serrated knives, an apple corer/slicer, a stove or hot plate, a medium-sized bowl, a large spoon, small bowls for serving, small plastic spoons for serving and eating, large paper cups for each child, stiff paper cut into strips, and four or five pictures of each ingredient below.

Ingredients: Applesauce (about 1/3 cup per child); unsweetened coconut, bananas, oranges, granola, raisins, and chopped nuts for toppings; a shaker of cinnamon or nutmeg, and lemon or vanilla yogurt (optional).

GETTING READY

Prepare the applesauce. Place apples in a large pot filled with water. Talk about how the apples float and bob up and down as children clean them. Help children peel the apples and cut them using the corer/slicer. Then place the apple pieces back in the pot. Add enough water so the pieces are covered one fourth of the way. Cook 15 to 20 minutes (depending on variety, ripeness, and firmness). As the apples cook, encourage children to observe and smell them.

BEGIN

Ask children to help you set up for a special snack. Together, pour the applesauce into a medium-sized bowl, and put in a serving spoon. Peel the bananas and oranges and cut them into small pieces. Place the unsweetened coconut, granola, raisins, chopped nuts, yogurt, and cut fruits into separate small bowls, each with a plastic spoon. Set the bowls on a table and add small shakers of cinnamon or nutmeg. Put out plastic spoons and large cups to hold individual sundaes. On another table, put out the paper strips, glue, and pictures of ingredients.

Talk about sundaes — what they are and what goes into them. Explain that today children will make applesauce sundaes, using picture recipes they invent themselves. Together, remember times your group used picture recipes to cook something.

Offer each child a paper strip and point out the pictures of ingredients. Ask children to decide which ingredients they want on their sundaes. Then glue those pictures in a row on their paper strips. They may want to look at the ingredients again and taste unfamiliar ones. Now offer encouragement as they follow their own picture recipe to assemble an applesauce sundae!

BOOKS

Here are books about people who cook for a living.

- *Marge's Diner* by Gail Gibbons (Thomas Y. Crowell)
- *Little Nino's Pizzeria* by Karen Barbour (Harcourt Brace Jovanovich)
- *My Father's Luncheonette* by Melanie Hope Greenberg (E.P. Dutton)

COOKING

Bake seeds and make shakes with this versatile vegetable!

PUMPKIN, PUMPKIN

Aim: Children will practice observation, descriptive language, and measuring skills.

Group Size: Four or five children.

Materials: Experience-chart paper and a marker; an oven; a small saucepan, a mixing bowl, a cookie sheet, and a blender; paper towels; measuring cups and spoons; paper cups and napkins for each child; and a sharp knife for adult use.

Ingredients: 2 cups milk, 2 bananas, 4 tbsp. canned pumpkin, 1/4 tsp. cinnamon (makes four 4-oz. shakes); one fresh pumpkin; 1-2 tablespoons butter or margarine; and Worcestershire sauce (optional).

BEGIN

Gather in a circle and invite children to watch as you cut off the top of a fresh pumpkin. Pass around the opened pumpkin. Encourage children to use their senses to observe the pumpkin, then describe it. Record their responses on experience-chart paper next to their names: Anthony — "It's round and bumpy." Arielle — "When I tap it, it sounds like 'Thud.'" Jonel — "The seeds feel slimy." Niki — "I like the way it smells."

Now pass around the canned pumpkin. Use your senses again to compare it to fresh. Add a second list to your chart describing the canned pumpkin. Talk about what might have been done to a fresh pumpkin to make it "turn into" canned.

Make a Pumpkin, Pumpkin Snack

Preheat an oven to 300 degrees. Melt 1-2 tablespoons butter or margarine in a small saucepan. Together, pull the insides from your fresh pumpkin and separate seeds from string. Rinse the seeds in warm water. Mix them in a bowl with the melted butter or margarine. If you choose, you could add about 1/8 teaspoon Worcestershire sauce. Spread the mixture out on a cookie sheet and bake about 20 minutes or until brown.

As the seeds bake, begin making pumpkin milk shakes. Together, measure the milk, canned pumpkin, and cinnamon into a blender. Peel and slice the bananas. Add them to the mixture and blend until foamy. Pour the shakes into paper cups. Serve them with roasted pumpkin seeds and graham crackers.

Remember

- Measuring is an important math skill. As you measure, talk about the different tools you use and compare amounts.
- Working with fresh pumpkin can be messy. Cover your work space with paper, and keep plenty of damp paper towels on hand. Some children might like to wear smocks.

BOOKS

Read these vegetable books with your five-year-olds.

- *Pumpkin Blanket* by Deborah Turney Zagwyn (Celestial Arts)
- *The Rosy Fat Magenta Radish* by Janet Wolf (Little, Brown)
- *Pumpkin, Pumpkin* by Jeanne Titherington (Scholastic)

ACTIVITY PLAN INDEX:
TWOS AND THREES

DEVELOPMENTAL AREAS AND SKILLS ENHANCED	COOPERATING AND SHARING	DEVELOPING SELF-CONFIDENCE	FINE-MOTOR SKILLS	GROSS-MOTOR SKILLS	EMERGENT LITERACY	SCIENCE PROCESS SKILLS	MATHEMATICAL SKILLS	HEALTHY EATING	PROBLEM-SOLVING SKILLS	DECISION-MAKING SKILLS	CREATIVE EXPRESSION
2'S ACTIVITY PLANS											
SANDWICH LOGS PAGE 38	■	■	■	■	■	■		■		■	
FUNNY-FACE PANCAKE SNACK PAGE 39	■	■	■	■	■		■	■	■	■	■
FIVE-SENSE APPLESAUCE PAGE 40	■	■	■	■	■	■		■			■
GO BANANAS! PAGE 41	■	■	■	■	■	■	■	■			
MAKING MUFFINS PAGE 42	■	■	■	■	■	■		■		■	
FRUIT DIPPERS PAGE 43	■	■	■	■	■	■		■		■	■
HAVE A TASTING PARTY! PAGE 44	■	■	■	■	■	■		■		■	
HOLD A TOAST BUFFET! PAGE 45	■	■	■	■	■	■		■		■	■
JIGGLING GELATIN PAGE 46	■	■	■	■	■	■		■			■
PERSONAL PIZZAS PAGE 47	■	■	■	■	■	■		■		■	■
3'S ACTIVITY PLANS											
MOUTHFULS OF MELON! PAGE 48	■	■	■	■	■	■		■		■	
LET'S MAKE PEANUT BUTTER PAGE 49	■	■	■	■	■	■	■	■	■	■	
SNACKING ON BREAD AND JAM PAGE 50	■	■	■	■	■	■	■	■			
ONE POTATO, TWO POTATO PAGE 51	■	■	■	■	■	■	■	■			
DEVILED EGG NESTS PAGE 52	■	■	■	■	■	■	■	■		■	■
CHEESE FEAST, ANYONE? PAGE 53	■	■	■	■	■	■		■		■	
TEA FOR TWO PAGE 54	■	■	■	■	■	■	■	■			■
YUMMY YOGURT SUNDAES PAGE 55	■	■	■	■	■	■		■		■	■
LET'S MAKE SNACK SHAPES PAGE 56	■	■	■	■	■	■	■			■	
FRIENDSHIP FRUIT SALAD PAGE 57	■	■	■	■				■		■	

ACTIVITY PLAN INDEX:
FOURS AND FIVES

DEVELOPMENTAL AREAS AND SKILLS ENHANCED	COOPERATING AND SHARING	DEVELOPING SELF-CONFIDENCE	FINE-MOTOR SKILLS	GROSS-MOTOR SKILLS	EMERGENT LITERACY	SCIENCE PROCESS SKILLS	MATHEMATICAL SKILLS	HEALTHY EATING	PROBLEM-SOLVING SKILLS	DECISION-MAKING SKILLS	CREATIVE EXPRESSION
4'S ACTIVITY PLANS											
WHOLE WHEAT SCONES **PAGE 58**	■	■	■	■	■	■	■	■			
SPIN A SALAD **PAGE 59**	■	■	■	■	■	■	■	■	■		
DESIGNING PRETZELS **PAGE 60**	■	■	■	■	■		■	■		■	■
NUTS! **PAGE 61**	■	■	■		■	■	■	■	■	■	
A MUSICAL COOKING ASSEMBLY LINE **PAGE 62**	■	■	■	■				■		■	■
THE HUNGRY CATER-PILLAR FRUIT SALAD **PAGE 63**	■	■	■	■	■	■	■	■	■	■	■
FRIENDSHIP SOUP **PAGE 64**	■	■	■	■	■			■		■	
HOW MANY WAYS CAN YOU SCRAMBLE AN EGG? **PAGE 65**	■	■	■	■	■	■		■	■	■	
HAVE A BREAD-TASTING PARTY **PAGE 66**	■	■	■	■	■	■	■	■			
SAUCE, BUTTER, CIDER, JUICE **PAGE 67**	■	■	■	■	■	■	■			■	
5'S ACTIVITY PLANS											
FRUIT SHAKES **PAGE 68**	■	■	■	■	■		■	■	■	■	
BROILED FRUIT CRISP **PAGE 69**	■	■	■	■	■	■	■	■	■		
HEALTHY FRUIT AND NUT GORP **PAGE 70**	■	■	■	■	■	■	■	■			
CREATE A GROUP SALAD BAR **PAGE 71**	■	■	■	■	■		■	■		■	■
WHAT CAN YOU DO WITH A BANANA? MAKE ICE CREAM! **PAGE 72**	■	■	■	■	■	■		■		■	■
MAKE YOUR OWN SNACK MIX **PAGE 73**	■	■	■	■	■	■	■	■	■	■	■
MASHED POTATO PUZZLE **PAGE 74**	■	■	■	■	■		■	■	■	■	■
YUMMY CARROT VEGETABLE SOUP **PAGE 75**	■	■	■	■	■			■	■		
RECIPE BY ME! **PAGE 76**	■	■	■	■	■	■	■		■	■	■
PUMPKIN, PUMPKIN **PAGE 77**	■	■	■	■	■	■	■	■	■		

RESOURCES

The following is a list of resource books, including cookbooks with nutritious, easy-to-use recipes for young children; nutrition resources for adults who want to learn more about serving healthy foods; curriculum aids for cooking with preschoolers; and children's picture books about food, eating, and cooking. Look for them in professional resource libraries at colleges and teachers' or children's bookstores.

COOKBOOKS
▼ *Cook and Learn: Pictorial Single Portion Recipes* by Thelma Harms and Beverly Veitch (Addison Wesley)
▼ *Crunchy Bananas* by Barbara Wilms (Redleaf Press)
▼ *Cup Cooking: Individual Child Portion Picture Recipes* by Barbara Johnson (Early Educators Press)
▼ *Fancy, Sweet, and Sugar Free* by Karen E. Barkie (St. Martin's Press)
▼ *The Good for Me Cookbook* by Karen B. Croft (R&E Research Assoc.)
▼ *Kids Are Natural Cooks* (Parents Nursery School, Cambridge, Mass.)
▼ *The Little Cooks: Recipes From Around the World*, adapted and illustrated by Eve Tharlet (Unicef)
▼ *Recipes to Grow On* by Central Minnesota Child Care, Inc. (Sun Ray Publishing)
▼ *Super Snacks* by Jean Warren (Gryphon House)
▼ *The Whole Child Cookbook*, edited by Jenene G. Carey and Dorothy Wilson (Summit Child Care Centers)

NUTRITION
▼ *Creative Food Experiences for Young Children* by Mary T. Goodwin and Gerry Pollen (Center for Public Interest)
▼ *Food: Early Choices Kit* by the National Dairy Council, 6300 North River Road, Rosemont, IL 60018
▼ *More Than Graham Crackers* by Nancy Wanamaker, Kristen Hearn, and Sherrill Richarz (NAEYC)

▼ *Nutrition Education for Young Children* by Carol Whitener & Marie Keeling (Redleaf Press)

COOKING WITH CHILDREN
▼ *Concept Cookery* by Kathy Faggella (First Teacher)
▼ *Cooking and Eating With Children* by O. McAfee (ACEI)
▼ "Cooking With Preschoolers," *The Wonder of It: Exploring How the World Works* by Bonnie Neugebauer (Exchange Press)
▼ *Learning Through Cooking* by Nancy J. Ferreira (Redleaf Press)
▼ *Meals Without Squeals* by Christine Berman & Jacki Fromer (Bull Publishing Company)

CHILDREN'S BOOKS
▼ *Anna's Goodbye Apron* by Julie Brillhart (Albert Whitman)
▼ *Bread, Bread, Bread* by Ann Morris (Lothrop, Lee & Shepard)
▼ *Gregory, the Terrible Eater* by Mitchell Sharmat (Macmillan)
▼ *Let's Eat* by Gyo Fujikawa (Grosset & Dunlap)
▼ *Max's Breakfast* by Rosemary Wells (Dial Books for Young Children)
▼ *Mealtime Photographs* by Stephen Shot (E.P. Dutton)
▼ *What a Good Lunch!* by Shigeo Watanabe (W. Collins Publishers)